I THESSALONIANS
A Commentary

7.50

ORTHODOX BIBLICAL STUDIES

I THESSALONIANS
A Commentary

by
PAUL NADIM TARAZI

ST. VLADIMIR'S SEMINARY PRESS
CRESTWOOD, NEW YORK
1982

Library of Congress Cataloging in Publication Data

Tarazi, Paul Nadim, 1943-
   I Thessalonians: a commentary.

   (Orthodox Biblical studies)
   Text of I Thessalonians in Greek with an English translation.
   Includes index.
   1. Bible. N.T. Thessalonians, 1st—Commentaries.
I. Bible. N.T. Thessalonians, 1st. English. Revised
Standard. 1982. II. Title. III. Series.
BS2725.3.T37   1982   227'.81077   82-16952
ISBN 0-913836-97-4

I THESSALONIANS
A Commentary

© Copyright 1982

by

PAUL NADIM TARAZI

ISBN 0-913836-97-4

PRINTED IN THE UNITED STATES OF AMERICA

BY

ATHENS PRINTING COMPANY
New York, NY 10001

To Costi Bendaly
a disciple of Jesus the Christ
a master of many
and
in loving memory of
Marcel, his brother
Jamal, my father
Widad, my mother
Raja, my godson

"whom we shall not precede" (I Thess. 4:15)

CONTENTS

PREFACE

The present book is the fruit of a vision. Unlike a program which tends to dictate the future, a vision is shaped by the morrow, it is open-armed; it embraces inasmuch as it is embraced. A program is successful or not, whereas a vision is fruitful or not. Success is our handiwork, while fruits are a gift like creation itself. Failure shatters our being; the lack of fruits produces patience which is an essential feature of a hopeful being, awaiting fulfillment . . . the lack of fruits is as creative as their plentifulness.

I shall not therefore endeavor to discuss the why or the how of such a commentary. I shall, however, say that the way it now stands is intended: the shortness of the introduction; the lack of bibliographical footnotes; the concentration on the biblical text itself and its movement; the extensive study of the words in both their meaning and their function in the sentence; the conception of a three-leveled exegesis included in the one main text of the commentary (see further below); the high importance, even centrality, given to the original Greek text . . .

The reader is invited to realize that the biblical text which we are dealing with is old and thus requires extremely attentive study to understand the exact meaning intended by its author. Moreover, this meaning is vital to our faith since the New Testament books are one of our closest witnesses to Jesus of Nazareth, the Messiah and the Lord.

I hope that I have offered the reader all the pertinent data for him to make up his own mind as to whether my interpretation is correct or not. To say this is to invite him to realize that the truth of our faith is linked to the correct and objective meaning of the actual text, and in no way on our personal preferences. He is not to be satisfied with the accommodating statement: "You have your understanding, I have mine; each one sees things his own way." Actually what matters is the Apostle Paul's meaning, and that can only be *one*. Whenever the reader disagrees with the present author, he is to realize that either both are wrong, or one of us is right, but that we cannot both be right.

Therefore, I beg him to follow as closely as possible the following steps:

1) Read carefully the first epistle to the Thessalonians in the Bible two or three times.

2) Only then read the first level of my commentary, comprised in the large-type text. The reader will soon find that it is a continuous work without any breaks.

3) Then read the second level of the commentary, *i.e.*, the medium-type text along with the large-type, as one continuous text. If you find any difficulties refer to a more knowledgeable person or study it in a group.

4) The third level will be the entire commentary. The part printed in the smallest type presupposes a good knowledge of Greek as well as of biblical criticism.

Regarding the English translation, I have opted for the most commonly used one: the Revised Standard Version. Whenever I felt that it was inaccurate or wanting, I have tried to include my own, sometimes by using more than one word or expression to render the original Greek.

Now that the present commentary is finally a reality seven years after I took up the pen, I cannot but recall the many, many faces I am indebted to: my teachers; my students; the many authors whose works I have read; all those people— not least among whom my colleagues, the priests and educators—whose constant request that I write biblical com-

mentaries have made out of me, a man of the spoken word,
a writer; the little children who, unintentionally, made me
taste the reality of the eucharist as well as understand better
the Apostle Paul, whenever I had to tell them, so full of
life, that the good news of the life-giving resurrection is
none but the message of the life-giving cross. They are all
responsible for the brighter segments of this book.

Yet I would be amiss if I did not expressly acknowledge
the following: First on the list are my brothers Nabil and
Nouhad. The lengthy philosophical, religious and theological
discussions I had with them, as well as their commitment to
the Church, have taught me a lot. Besides, being both older
than I, the sound of "Father Paul" on their lips has a particular resonance. To them I owe a lasting recognition.

My special gratitude goes to His Eminence, Metropolitan
Philip, Primate of the Antiochian Orthodox Christian Archdiocese of North America, for having relieved me of my
pastoral duties to dedicate myself to writing a series of biblical
commentaries. I am grateful to the Board of Trustees of the
archdiocese for having endorsed His Eminence's suggestion
that I be alloted a yearly grant out of the general budget to
help take care of my material needs. I am grateful as well to
the members of the Order of St. Ignatius of Antioch of the
same archdiocese for having graciously accepted to endorse
the securing of this grant as one of their commitments.

More than once when, on the table loaded with Bibles
and concordances, my right hand found enough space to jot
the words that became the present book, my left arm was
holding either Jalal, my son, or Reem, my daughter, rocking
them to sleep. My wife once took a picture of me with Reem.

Bassam, my baby boy, was the only one who actually enjoyed the mess in my study. He was allowed to wander freely
there and thus be close to his daddy whenever he wished
without threatening the course of my thoughts.

Imkje, my wife, has been by far the greatest challenge to
my theological thinking. Years later a former statement of

mine is brought up in the course of a conversation to question my new position. She is indeed a companion. Yet, the other face of her challenge to me is that, while I am often struggling with the written words in the Bible to get to the heart of its message, she so eloquently lives daily that love for the neighbor that encompasses the entire good news. Often when I question the feasibility of Christianity, her presence dissipates my doubts.

INTRODUCTION

Silvanus and Timothy

In the opening greeting of both epistles to the Thessalonians, the Apostle Paul includes the names of Silvanus and Timothy. Who were they?

Silvanus, together with Timothy, is mentioned a third time by Paul in II Cor. 1:19: "For the Son of God, Jesus Christ, whom we preached among you, Silvanus and Timothy and I, was not Yes and No; but in him it is always Yes." Thus we know from the Pauline correspondence that this Silvanus was active with Paul in Philippi (I Thess. 1:2), Thessalonica and Corinth. Now these three cities were the main stops in Paul's second missionary journey (Acts 14:40-18:22), where we read about a certain Silas whose name appears twelve or thirteen[1] times between 15:22-18:5. This Silas was Paul's main companion (see 15:40)[2] during this journey and his mention in Acts is restricted to it. There is thus no doubt that Silvanus and Silas are one and same person.[3] From Acts 15 we learn that he was a leading figure (v.22), more specifically a prophet (v.32) in the early church. The person and office of such prophets can be seen

---

[1]Acts 15:34, "But it seemed good to Silas to remain there," is a doubtful text.

[2]He is frequently mentioned with Paul during their activity in Philippi and Thessalonica, whereas Timothy is not cited at all.

[3]Starting with the Hellenistic period many Jews used two names: one Hebrew and the other Greek. Let us mention the best known cases in the New Testament: Simon/Peter, Saul/Paul, John/Mark.

particularly clearly in I Corinthians. They were considered
the chief leaders after the apostles (see I Cor. 12:28 and
Eph. 4:11). Sometime after Paul's second missionary journey Silvanus/Silas seems to have joined Peter, as appears
from I Pet. 5:12: "By Silvanus, a faithful brother as I regard
him, I have written briefly to you ..."

The reader of the New Testament will easily notice that,
starting with the Book of Acts, the name which is most
frequently mentioned, besides Paul and Peter, is that of
Timothy (twenty-four times). The same reader will quite
as easily remark that most of these instances (eighteen times)
appear in the literature ascribed to Paul, whereas his mention in Acts is always in conjunction with Paul's missionary
activity.[4] Starting with Paul's decision to appoint him as
companion at the recommendation of the brethren at Lystra,
his home town (Acts 16:1-3), Timothy became not only
the permanent colleague of the great apostle (Acts 17:14-
15; 18:5; 19:2; 20:4; Rom. 16:21; II Cor. 1:1, 19; Phil.
1:1; Col. 1:1; I Thess. 1:1; II Thess. 1:1; Philem. 1), but
also his most valuable coadjutant, to whom he assigned
touchy missions (I Cor. 4:17; 16:10; I Thess. 3:2, 6). On
one occasion the imprisoned Paul laid open his inner feelings: "I hope in the Lord Jesus to send *Timothy* to you
soon, so that I may be cheered by news of you. *I have no one
like him*, who will be *genuinely anxious for your welfare*.
They all look after their own interests, not those of Jesus
Christ. But *his* (*viz.* Timothy's) *worth you know*, how *as a
son with a father he has served with me* in the gospel"
(Phil. 2:19-22). Later we find Timothy, bishop of Ephesus,
addressed as "my true child in the faith" (I Tim. 1:2),
"my son" (I Tim. 1:18), and "my beloved child" (II Tim.
1:1). Timothy: a modest beginning, a great life in Christ's
service. One may rightly wonder whether Paul's missionary
activity would have been as fruitful as it was had it not

---

[4]Acts 16:1; 17:14-15; 19:22; 20:4.

been for Timothy's handling of delicate issues on his behalf when the apostle to the Gentiles was too busy to undertake such missions. At any rate, we today are indebted to the brethren of Lystra and Iconium for their witness and recommendation (Acts 16:2) and should pray that God grant the same spirit of seriousness to all those among us put in a position of recommending someone to a ministry in the church.

The Stay at Thessalonica

Silvanus/Silas and Timothy accompanied Paul on his second missionary journey which took him to the Roman provinces of Macedonia and Achaia (both located in present-day Greece). Their respective capitals were Thessalonica and Corinth. Now, all introductions to our epistle refer to discrepancies between the data of Acts and those of I Thess. There is no doubt that Paul's letter contains first-hand information, and thus every study of the issue must start with it and give it priority whenever there is any contradiction. However, before rushing to conclude that the Book of Acts yields incorrect or inaccurate information, one must remember that, due to the scale of its scope, Acts is intended to be programmatic and in no way detailed.

Now, from the text of I Thess. we can gather the following information regarding the Apostle's stay in Thessalonica:

1) Paul, Silvanus and Timothy were all involved in the evangelization of Thessalonica (1:1, 5, 9; 2:1).

2) They came there from Philippi (another main city of Macedonia), where they had been mistreated (2:2); and after they met a great opposition there (2:2-5) Paul proceeded to Athens in Achaia (3:1).

3) In Thessalonica they stayed some time (2:9), perhaps even a long time (2:7-8, 10-11); and the main bulk of the Thessalonian Christians seem to be of heathen origin (1:9; 4:3-5; 4:13).

4) These Christians have physically suffered from their fellow citizens (1:6; 2:14). One might guess from 2:14 that the Jews of Thessalonica were behind this upheaval. The guess is confirmed from our detailed study of the words used in 2:3 and 5.

A study of Acts will immediately show that it closely follows the above data:

1) Silas/Silvanus was Paul's main companion in Thessalonica (17:1-15, especially vv.4 and 10) as well as in Philippi (16:11-40, especially vv.19, 25 and 29). As for Timothy, his mention in 16:1 and later in 17:14-15 and 18:5 proves beyond any doubt that he too shared in the evangelization of those cities. See further below.

2) The sequence Philippi—Thessalonica—Athens is parallel to that in Acts (16:11-40; 17:1-15; 17:15-18:1). The shameful and insulting treatment suffered by Paul in Philippi and mentioned by Paul in I Thess. 2:2 is elucidated in Acts 16:22-23, 36-39. The great opposition of I Thess. 2:2 is also clarified in Acts 17:5-10.

3) The length of the Thessalonian stay is actually the cornerstone of the attack among biblical critics against the accuracy of the information we find in Acts. They suggest that according to Acts (17:2) Paul stayed a maximum of three weeks and that his main activity took place among the Jews; whereas I Thess. tells us that the majority of the Christians there were originally heathen and indicates that they knew a lot about the Old Testament and the Christian faith by the time Paul left. Three weeks is considered too short a period to have produced such results.[5]

4) That the Thessalonian Christians suffered at the hand of their fellow-citizens at the instigation of the Jews is to be found in Acts 17:5-9.

---

[5]The spreading of the news regarding the faith of the Thessalonians (1:8) and the worry provoked by the rather large number of deaths in the community (4:13-14) are noted against the assumed shortness of Paul's stay in Thessalonica.

Thus, if we can shed some light on the issue of the length of Paul's stay in Thessalonica, much can be said concerning the reliability of Acts. In Acts 17:1-4 we read: "Now when they had passed through Amphipolis and Apolonia, they came to Thessalonica, *where there was a synagogue of the Jews. And as was his custom*—κατὰ δὲ τὸ εἰωϑὸς—Paul went to them—εἰσῆλϑεν πρὸς αὐτοὺς—and on three sabbaths—ἐπὶ σάββατα τρία—he argued—διελέξατο— with them from the scriptures—ἀπὸ τῶν γραφῶν, explaining and proving that it was necessary for Christ to suffer and to rise from the dead, and saying, 'This Jesus, whom I proclaim to you, is the Christ.' And some of them were persuaded, and joined Paul and Silas; as did a great many of the devout Greeks and not a few of the leading women." Indeed, Paul's custom was to start his mission in a given city by going on the sabbath day to the local synagogue— where there was one (see Acts 16:13)—and preaching there to the Jews (13:13, 42, 44; 16:13; 18:4). Sometimes he was invited to come again once (13:42, 44) or even more (18:5).

If the Jews were dissatisfied with his teachings they would expel him from the synagogue (13:45, 50). In this case Paul would settle in one of the houses graciously put at his disposal and make out of it his headquarters (Acts 16:14-16; 18:2-3, 7). Such houses became with time the regular meeting places for the new communities of the believers in Jesus Christ, *i.e.*, for the churches (Rom. 16:5/ I Cor. 16:19; Col. 4:15; Philem. 2). Such was the residence of Jason (Acts 17:5-9) where the Jews knew that Paul would be.

Consequently there is no need to understand Acts 17:2 as meaning that Paul and his companions stayed only three weeks in Thessalonica. It means simply that they preached only three sabbaths at the synagogue. Then they were forced to move into the house of Jason. There, Paul may have stayed a longer time and gathered quite a number of believers, mainly from among the Gentiles. Paul's success was precisely what triggered the Jews' jealousy. Thus the writer of Acts might be much more accurate than many critics imagine.

His accuracy is further reflected in a very interesting feature in his account of the Thessalonian ministry. Though Timothy is introduced in 16:1, he is not mentioned at all throughout Paul's and Silas' activity in both Philippi and Thessalonica. His name reappears in 17:14-15 where we read that Silas and he remained in Beroea while Paul proceeded to Athens, after all three had fled Thessalonica. The explanation is simple: Timothy was just a meager figure compared to the Apostle Paul and the prophet Silas; he was just an apprentice and his role amounted to practically nothing at Philippi and Thessalonica. But why would his name suddenly appear along with that of Silas in Beroea?

The very immediate answer is that, Paul being absent, Silas moved from the second place to the first while Timothy became his main helper. We believe that there is more to it. In I Thess. 3:1-2 Paul writes that he was willing to remain *alone* in Athens and send Timothy to check on the Thessalonians' faith. "Alone" means that Silas was still in Beroea. This is how we imagine things went. Upon his arrival in Athens, Paul sent back his companions to Beroea with an order that Silas and Timothy should follow him as soon as possible (Acts 17:15). But the situation of the new Christians seems to have remained difficult in Beroea—otherwise why would Paul have left his companions there in the first place (Acts 17:14)?—as well as in Thessalonica (I Thess. 2:17-3:10). Silas remained in Beroea to keep an eye on both communities. Timothy came to Athens to bring Paul up-to-date on the situation. Although he was experiencing rough times in this city (Acts 17:32-34) and needed a companion, he realized the need of the Thessalonians for Timothy and accepted to send him to the Macedonian capital. With this his first mission this young disciple proved to be up to the delicate mission entrusted to him and worthy of his being mentioned along with Silas in 17:14-15 and 18:5.

Paul's Opponents

The author of Acts has been accused—falsely to our mind—of being too much biased in presenting the Jews as systematically hindering Paul's work, even persecuting him. Many theories have been formulated to explain this so-called phenomenon, which moreover was adduced as an argument against that author's accuracy. Paul's comments in I Cor., II Cor., Gal. and Phil. should be enough to convince us of the systematic opposition the Jews showed him. As for their persecuting him, his mention of having received at their hands five times the forty lashes less one (I Cor. 11:24) as well as the danger he encountered from his own people (11:26) should be enough to support it.[6] Still, our detailed exegesis of I Thess. 2:3-6 and 14-16[7] will show that Acts 17:1-15 undoubtedly reflects historical facts. It will also reveal that, already in his first correspondence to a church, Paul makes it clear that the staunchest opponents to his gospel message had been and still were the Jews.

Place and Date of I Thess.

I Thess. 2:17-3:13 shows beyond any doubt not only that Paul was extremely worried about the Thessalonians, but also that he had not left them long before. This suggests that the letter was written in the course of the second missionary journey, sometime after the founding of the church

---

[6]One can also add the escape from Damascus in a basket (vv.32-33), since there is no reason to doubt the account in Acts 9:23-25 which states that the Jews were behind such a plot.

[7]Some critics today consider vv.14-16 a later addition. However, their case has been proved untenable.

in Thessalonica. Besides, the mention of Athens occurs, in addition to I Thess. 3:1, only in Acts 17:15-18-1 (several times), that is between Beroea and Corinth during this journey. Now, I Thess. was written after Timothy's return from Thessalonica (3:6) to Corinth (Acts 18:5), where Paul stayed eighteen months (18:11). Corinth is thus the most plausible place where our epistle was written.

From Acts 18:12 we learn that Gallio became proconsul of Achaia when Paul was still residing in Corinth. An inscription discovered at Delphi in Greece, which contains a copy of a letter of the Emperor Claudius to Gallio, helps us to determine quite accurately that this proconsul held office in Corinth between July 1, 51, and June 30, 52.[8] Now Acts 18:12 tells us that the Jews were not able to unite their attack against Paul except with the advent of the new proconsul Gallio, whereas 18:18 indicates that after Gallio's arrival Paul remained in Corinth many days longer ἔτι ἡμέρας ἱκανάς. Since it is not clear how long a period these many days were, Paul must have written his letter either in the latter half of 50 or the first half of 51. We opt for the year 50 because all the indications point towards some time immediately after the arrival of Timothy in Corinth.

---

[8]Incidentally, the time of Gallio's proconsulate in Corinth is one of the very rare accurate extra-biblical dates upon which sound New Testament chronology is to be built.

CHAPTER ONE

v.1. Παῦλος καὶ Σιλουανὸς καὶ Τιμό-
θεος τῇ ἐκκλησίᾳ Θεσσαλονικέων
ἐν Θεῷ πατρὶ καὶ κυρίῳ Ἰησοῦ
Χριστῷ· χάρις ὑμῖν καὶ εἰρήνη.

Paul and Silvanus and Timothy, to the church of the Thessalonians in God the Father and the Lord Jesus Christ: grace to you and peace.

First-century A.D. epistolary literature had basic rules which were generally followed by everyone. The sender started by mentioning his name, then that of the addressee and finally used the traditional greeting formula. Thus, the heading of any letter sounded as follows: so-and-so to so-and-so says (sends, wishes) greeting (health, peace). The shortness of this introductory formula was usually compensated with extensive greetings and wishes included towards the end of the letter. The Apostle Paul was thus bound by the contemporary usage. But, as we shall soon see, that fact itself will allow us to realize how Paul was able to pour into this traditional literary mould a completely new content rooted in his Christian faith.

From the introductory formula we understand that the senders of the letter are three: the Apostle Paul and his adjutants in the founding of the church in Thessalonica, namely

21

Silvanus the prophet and young Timothy (see the Introduction). Still the question remains as to whether all three took part in the composition or wording of this letter, or the author was one—namely Paul—except that he included for reasons of protocol those who shared with him the hardships involved in the edification of a Christian community in the capital of Macedonia. In order to give an answer let us consider the following:

1) In spite of the fact that the overwhelming majority of the verbs used in I Thess. are in the plural, we still find obvious indications that Paul is the actual author: "So we wanted to come to you—I Paul, more than once" (2:18); "For this reason, when I could bear it no longer, I sent that I might know your faith" (3:5); "I adjure you by the Lord..." (5:27).

2) The same recurs in II Thess.: "Do you not remember that when I was still with you I told you this"? (2:5); "I Paul, write this greeting with my own hand. This is the mark in every letter of mine; it is the way I write" (3:17).

3) Paul abides by the same rule in his subsequent correspondence. See especially I Cor. and Phil. where he begins saying: "I give thanks to God..." despite the inclusion of Sosthenes the brother (I Cor. 1:1) and Timothy (Phil. 1:1) as co-senders.

It is then clear that Paul alone is the actual author of I Thess. as well as of the rest of his letters. This is precisely what tradition left us with; and the church teaches us the same thing whenever the reader chants in the midst of the assembled faithful: "A reading from the epistle of St. Paul to..." without mention of the other names included in the epistle's introductory greeting.

The addressee of the present letter is the church of the Thessalonians. A digression, though lengthy, is in order here since we consider it an integral part of the commentary. The word ἐκκλησία (church) does not originally mean the community in general, since the word δῆμος (people, the community of the people) is used in that instance. Ἐκκλησία describes the gathering, regular or extraordinary, held by the people to discuss matters concerning the welfare of the community. In other words, ἐκκλησία is the people gathered around its leaders and representatives in a meeting expressive of the unity, perhaps even the deep being, of such a people. Therefore, when the Jews of Alexandria—where we find the largest Jewish community outside Palestine after the fourth century B.C.—began the translation of the sacred scriptures from Hebrew into Greek starting around the mid-third century B.C.,[1] the translators used ἐκκλησία to render the Hebrew word *qahal*, whereas they usually rendered *'edah* with συναγωγή (synagogue). In the Old Testament *'edah* means the community of the people gathered in the presence of God, while by comparison *qahal* expresses more the fact of the gathering, that is the movement itself toward the meeting. *Qahal* bears therefore the meaning of the people being gathered at God's calling.[2] Now when the early church which used Greek called herself ἐκκλησία, she did so according to the meaning of this word as found in the Old Testament. It is essential to note here that *qahal*/ἐκκλησία was never used in its technical sense except to designate the community of Israel. Thus the expression "the church—ἡ ἐκκλησία" used absolutely meant the community of the faithful in Jerusalem, who were mostly of Jewish extraction. This explains why, although the gospel news had spread

---

[1]This translation is called Septuagint and its symbol is LXX. See Appendix I for further details.

[2]The apostles' preference for the use of ἐκκλησία over συναγωγή goes back in our view to the following reasons: (a) first-century A.D. Jews were using συναγωγή to speak of their religious meetings as well as of the buildings where these gatherings took place; (b) the word ἐκκλησία was well known to the Gentiles who used it for their public meetings; (c) ἐκκλησία has the same root as the adjective "κλητός—chosen" which was a technical term indicating every Christian believer in that he was chosen by God and thus became a member of the holy community.

beyond Palestine, we read in Acts 12:1-5: "About that time
Herod the king laid violent hands upon some who belonged
to *the church*. He killed James the brother of John with the
sword; and when he saw that it pleased the Jews, he proceeded
to arrest Peter also. This was during the days of unleavened
bread. And when he had seized him, he put him in prison,
and delivered him to four squads of soldiers to guard him,
intending after the passover to bring him out to the people.
So Peter was kept in prison; but earnest prayer for him
was made to God by *the church*." There is no doubt that "the
church" in vv.1 and 5 refers to the church of Jerusalem, on the
basis of the following considerations:

1) Herod[3] was king over Palestine and his capital was
evidently Jerusalem;

2) If Herod was able to kill the brother of John and
have Peter arrested, it is because the apostles were still in
Jerusalem and not yet scattered;

3) The mention that Peter's arrest occurred during the
days of unleavened bread and that Herod had him jailed
until after the passover[4] cannot be understood unless those
events happened in a place where the passover celebration
was of special importance. Now, that would have applied
only to Jerusalem, where this celebration was at its brightest
in the temple;

4) Even if we assume that Peter was seized on the first
day of the unleavened bread and that he was miraculously

---

[3]Herod Agrippa I, son of Herod the Great's son Aristobulus. He was
the brother of Herodias (Mt. 14:3; Mk. 6:17; Lk. 3:19) and the father
of Herod Agrippa II, in whose presence the Apostle Paul appeared in
Jerusalem (Acts 25:23-16:32). He reigned over Judea and Samaria between
41 and 44 A.D.

[4]The feast of unleavened bread lasted seven days, while the passover
commemoration took place on the eve of the first day and thus was itself
a meal of unleavened bread. Thus in the New Testament era the two feasts
were practically integrated into a single festivity, so that either term referred
to the whole period. This clarifies the apparent inconsistency in the text
where we read that Peter, who was jailed during the days of "unleavened
bread," was not to be brought out to the people until after the passover.

rescued from jail on the last night of this period—since Herod was planning to bring him out to the people the following day (compare vv.4 and 6)—this would mean that the apostle was jailed for a maximum period of seven days.[5] It is impossible to imagine that the entire church all over the evangelized areas of the Roman Empire would have become aware of Peter's imprisonment in such a short period.

Moreover, we find in the Book of Acts another text that confirms our position: "When he (*i.e.*, Paul) had landed in Caesarea, he *went up* and greeted *the church*, and then went down to Antioch" (18:22). Here again "the church" definitely means the community of the faithful in the city of Jerusalem. Indeed:

1) The verb "to go up" is well known to be used in conjunction with Jerusalem[6] for the obvious reason that this city lies on top of one of the most elevated Judean hills. Its visitor has "to go up" from virtually whatever direction he is coming. Besides, the idea of ascending to Jerusalem was already imbedded in biblical language since Old Testament times.

2) Paul used to visit the church in Jerusalem after each of his journeys and before returning to his headquarters in Antioch (Acts 21:4, 12, 15).

3) Again in the Book of Acts, when Paul was under arrest at the Roman governor Festus' residence in the city of Caesarea in Palestine, we read the following: "Now when Festus had come into his province, after three days he *went up to Jerusalem* from Caesarea ... But Festus, wishing to do the Jews a favor, said to Paul: "Do you wish to *go up to Jerusalem*, and there be tried on these charges before me?" (25:1 and 9).

However, this exclusive use of the expression "the church" did not hinder the apostles and their disciples from using the term "church" in order to designate Christian communities in

---

[5]See note 4 above.
[6]Acts 11:2; 13:31; 15:2; 21:4, 12, 15; 24:11; 25:1, 9.

other localities, even where the Gentile Christians far out-
numbered their brothers in the faith of Jewish extraction, as
was the case in Thessalonica.[7] And that is precisely the radical
change which took place in the person of Jesus Christ: the
Gentile nations that believed in Him became "churches" in
the same sense that qualified the community of the faithful
in Jerusalem, the Holy City, since the faith in Jesus Christ,
the baptism in His name and the gathering around His
precious body and blood in the eucharistic mystery, have become the criteria of the church's membership. Thus, the short
introductory greeting itself already bears the whole of the
Good News of salvation in Jesus Christ in the following
simple words: "to the church of the Thessalonians." For what
brighter message to the whole world could there be than to
have a bunch of idol worshippers (I Thess. 1:9) suddenly
called "church." The idol worshippers have become a church!
That is indeed the Good News, for the church—every church—
is the church of God. Thus the expression "the church of
the Thessalonians" actually means "the church of God which
is in Thessalonica." This is clearly shown in that the Apostle
writes to the Christians of that city: "For you, brethren, became imitators of the churches of God in Christ Jesus which
are—τῶν οὐσῶν—in Judea" (2:14). Thus, although she is
known by the name of a given place (I Cor. 16: 1, 9; II Cor.
8:1; Gal. 1:2, 22) or that of its inhabitants (Col. 4:16;
I Thess. 1:1; II Thess. 1:1), the church is but the one church
of God that takes a given aspect in a given place, in other
words, the church of God which is in such a city or province
(I Cor. 1:2; II Cor. 1:2; I Thess. 2:14; see also Rom. 16:1).

That is what made Paul qualify the church of the Thessalonians by adding: "in God the Father and the Lord Jesus
Christ." But this qualification itself carries a new teaching
unimaginable, then as well as now, to any Jewish reader

---

[7]This is reflected in the fact that the epistle seems to be addressed mainly
to Christians of Gentile extraction, as appears from I Thess. 1:9 and 2:14.

of the Old Testament, namely: the defining of the church
not only with reference to God or God the Father, but also
to the Lord Jesus Christ; even more: in some instances we
read that the church is simply "in Christ" (Gal. 1:22) or "in
Christ Jesus" (I Thess. 2:14) without mention of God the
Father. This is why Paul wrote once in all clarity that the
churches were "the churches of Christ" (Rom. 16:16). All
of the preceding shows that, since the beginning, the Lord
Jesus Christ was held by the faith of the early church in no
less honor than that given to God the Father. Moreover, the
use of the one preposition "in—ἐν" before God the Father
and the Lord Jesus Christ interlocks them in Paul's mind as
the one source of the church.

Could we still learn more from the correlation "God the
Father and the Lord Jesus Christ"? In the Old Testament
there is complete parallelism between the expressions "God"
and "the Lord" since both indicate God Himself. In the New
Testament we find some kind of differentiation in the use of
these names in that the first has become specific of God
the Father, whereas the second—which expresses more specifically the living God of the Old Testament[8]—is used especially of Jesus Christ. What New Testament reader does
not think of the Father when he sees the word "God—
Θεός" and remember Jesus when reading the word "the
Lord—κύριος"? That is precisely an outcome of the apostles'
ingenuity: they expressed thus their belief in Jesus Christ's
divinity without mixing His person and that of God the
Father.

But the text of our epistle invites us to a further step
since it conveys something regarding the relationship between
the Lord Jesus and God the Father. Paul tells us here that
the Lord is Jesus Christ,[9] that person whom the apostles lived
with and who was born in Bethlehem, grew up in Galilee,

---

[8]See the study of the word "Lord—κύριος" in Appendix II.
[9]See the study of the word "Christ—Χριστός" in Appendix III.

lived in Palestine preaching, teaching and performing miracles, and finally came to Jerusalem where he suffered, died, was buried and rose on the third day to sit in glory at His Father's right hand. As for God, the Apostle identifies Him as "the Father"; however, this expression in its turn needs more clarification since the word "father" expresses a relationship and is insufficient by itself. Now, this relationship of fatherhood is first and primarily with Jesus, since He was the only one to call God in all freedom "Abba—my Father" (Mk. 14:36). As for us, if we dare to call God "our Father," it is because He sent into our hearts the Spirit of His Son Jesus, who teaches us to call out in the same manner (Gal. 4:6 and Rom. 8:15-17). In other words, the church's faith in God is the same as her faith in Him as Father, the Father of Jesus Christ. And if that fatherhood is, as we showed, a definition of God, then God's fatherhood of Jesus is co-eternal with His divinity. Thus the teaching of the holy church is not only that God the Father and the Lord Jesus Christ are one God, but also that the former is Eternal Father and the latter Eternal Son.

Finally, Paul ends his introductory greeting with: "Grace to you and peace." As we mentioned above, this was the contemporary usage, namely that the author expresses this traditional salutation immediately after his name and that of his addressees. However, instead of the common χαῖρε or in the plural χαίρετε, which means: be glad, may you be glad and healthy, may you be whole . . . , Paul used the word χάρις, from the same root as the above-mentioned verb, but which has a special connotation in Christian literature: the grace that God bestows upon the believers for the salvation of each one of them and that produces in them the different gifts whose aim is the life of community in the Church. Thus χάρις is the source of the new kind of life specific of the Christians. Besides this grace, the Apostle wishes his readers that peace which is the result of the divine grace which God through His prophets has promised to implement at the end

of times. Thus this peace is not a human one, but rather
the true peace originating in God, the peace of God Himself.
All this shows that the church is aware that she is living in
the atmosphere of the end of the times, *i.e.*, in the full
presence of God, where all His promises are fulfilled. That
is why Paul wishes for every believer to share in this peace
according to his capacity. It is indeed to the extent that we
ourselves share in it and then share it with the others that the
world will taste the infinite love of God and consequently
that His kingdom—the kingdom of His love—will expand to
the whole world.

Finally, the expression "to you—ὑμῖν" indicates that Paul
used to address his letters to the gathered local community.
It thus seems that his epistles were read before all those present
at a religious gathering, and this habit spread in the churches
until our own day when, during the services, readings are
taken from the New Testament epistles. The Apostle himself left us with one text very clear in this respect: "And
when this letter has been read among you, have it read also
in the church of the Laodiceans; and see that you read also
the letter from Laodicea" (Col. 4:16).

v.2. Εὐχαριστοῦμεν τῷ Θεῷ πάντοτε
περὶ πάντων ὑμῶν, μνείαν ποιούμενοι ἐπὶ τῶν προσευχῶν ἡμῶν
ἀδιαλείπτως,

We give thanks to God always for you all,
constantly mentioning you in our prayers,

Following the literary usage of his time, Paul opened his
letters by offering thanks to God (Rom. 1:8; I Cor. 1:4;

Eph. 1:16; Phil. 1:3-4; Col. 1:3; I Thess. 1:2; II Thess. 1:3; Philem. 4; see also II Thess. 2:13).[10] However, he actually went beyond the common usage in that this his thanksgiving was an integral part of his constant prayer. Thus the importance of the adverb "always," which carries us into the Apostle's heart, a permanent altar for supplications whence ascended continually the good odor of his thanksgiving.

The importance of the idea of permanence in prayer in Paul's mind is reflected in the fact that out of the forty-one instances where the adverb "always—πάντοτε" is found in the New Testament, twenty-seven (i.e., ⅔) appear in his letters,[11] out of which eleven are in direct relationship either with prayer in general or with thanksgiving in particular (Rom. 1:10; I Cor. 1:4; *Eph. 5:20*; Phil. 1:4; Col. 1:3; 4:12; I Thess. 1:2; II Thess. 1:3, 11; 2:13; Philem. 4). Besides, this adverb is used in three[12] more passages where the idea is obviously that of prayer:

1) In I Thess. 3:6 we read: "But now that Timothy has come to us from you, and has brought us the good news of your faith and love and reported that you always—πάντοτε—remember (make remembrance)—ἔχετε μνείαν—us kindly and long to see us, as we long to see you," where πάντοτε appears in conjunction with "remembrance—μνεία." The latter word is found only seven times in the New Testament and all seven in Paul's letters. Now in the other six instances μνεία has the meaning of prayer.[13] Hence the kind/good remembrance in our verse is remembrance in prayer.

2) In I Thess. 5:16 we find πάντοτε with the verb "rejoice." But the context is obviously one of prayer: "Rejoice always, pray constantly, give thanks in all circumstances" (vv.16-18).

3) Paul's admonition to the Philippians: "Rejoice in the Lord al-

---

[10]With the exception of II Cor. 1:3; this exception will be discussed in our projected commentary on I Corinthians. As for Eph. 1:3, we do not consider it an exception since the thanksgiving prayer appears in v.16. This will also be discussed in an eventual commentary on Ephesians.

[11]We except Hebrews 7:25, since we consider that Paul himself did not write this letter.

[12]Four if we counted II Cor. 2:14: "χάρις be to God." However, the word χάρις here has the connotation of thankfulness ("thanks be to God") and does not mean grace.

[13]Rom. 1:9; Eph. 1:16; Phil. 1:3; I Thess. 1:2; II Tim. 1:3; Philem. 3.

[14]There is a very close literal parallelism between Phil. 4:5 and I Thess. 5:14-15; hence the atmosphere is the same.

ways—πάντοτε; again I will say, rejoice" (4:4) also runs parallel
to his exhorting them to prayer and thanksgiving: "Have no
anxiety about anything, but in everything by prayer and supplication
with thanksgiving let your requests be made known to God"
(4:6).[14]

By adding these three passages to our initial count, the outcome
is the following: in more than half of the instances (fourteen out
of twenty-seven) in which Paul uses the word πάντοτε, he does
so in conjunction with prayer.

Now the thanksgiving that Paul renders to God at the
beginning of his letters is always for the believers to whom
he is addressing himself (Rom. 1:8; I Cor. 1:4; Eph. 1:16;
Phil. 1:4; Col. 1:3, 9; I Thess. 1:2; II Thess. 1:3; 2:13) and
whose remembrance he makes in his prayers. And the use
of the word "remembrance—μνεία" by the Apostle always
in conjunction with prayer[15] is an indication that he used to
remember them personally and did not satisfy himself with
a general mention. His oneness and communion with the
other believers is rooted in their continual remembrance in
his prayers. Prayer in the life of the early church seems to
be the firmest bond between Christians particularly when it
is qualified by the personal mention of others as well as by
constancy or permanency, as is evident from the use of
"always—πάντοτε" and "constantly—ἀδιαλείπτως" in the
same verse.

There is an ongoing debate among scholars as to whether
the adverb ἀδιαλείπτως is to be taken with the expression "mentioning—μνείαν ποιούμενοι—you in our prayers," or should qualify
the present participle "remembering—μνημονεύοντες" that begins
the third verse. We incline towards the former alternative out of
the following considerations:

1) We find this word six times in the New Testament: four
as adverb ἀδιαλείπτως (Rom. 1:9; I Thess. 1:2; 2:13; 5:17) and
two as adjective ἀδιάλειπτος (Rom. 9:2; I Tim. 1:3), and all of
them at Paul's hand. Consequently the word is typically his.

---

[15]Rom. 1:9; Eph. 1:16; Phil. 1:3; I Thess. 1:2; 3:6; II Tim. 1:3;
Philem. 4.

2) In four[16] of these instances (all except Rom. 9:2) the subject is obvious: prayer. As for Rom. 9:2, there also the connection, though indirect, is definitely with prayer. To be sure, the complete text reads as follows: "I am speaking the truth in Christ, I am not lying; my conscience bears me witness in the Holy Spirit that I have great sorrow and unceasing—ἀδιάλειπτος—anguish in my heart. For I could wish—ηὐχόμην γάρ—that I myself were accursed and cut off from Christ for the sake of my brethren, my kinsmen by race" (Rom. 9:1-3). Here the Apostle expresses his unceasing pain in a prayer which must also have been constant, since (a) ηὐχόμην is from the verb εὔχομαι whose first meaning is: I pray, I supplicate, I ask . . . and consequently: I wish, I hope, I would love; (b) a wish of the kind encountered in Rom. 9:2 cannot be understood unless addressed to God in whose hand only lies the decision in such a matter, i.e., unless it is a prayer. Anyway, the Apostle's wish is comparable to what Moses had once done before him when he said to the Lord: "Alas, this people have sinned a great sin; they have made for themselves gods of gold. But now, if thou wilt forgive their sin—and if not, blot me, I pray thee, out of thy book which thou hast written" (Ex. 32:31-32); (c) ηὐχόμην is directly related to the unceasing—ἀδιάλειπτος—anguish through the conjunction γάρ which means: since, for. Our conclusion is that both words ἀδιαλείπτως and ἀδιάλειπτος are consistently used with the idea of prayer itself, and not with the reason or aim of such a prayer, which would be the case if we linked ἀδιαλείπτως of I Thess. 1:2 to the following verse.

3) The objection raised against the use of both adverbs πάντοτε and ἀδιαλείπτως in the same sentence can be easily dismissed, since (a) each of the two adverbs refers to a different verb: the former, to "we give thanks—εὐχαριστοῦμεν," and the latter to the present participle "making—ποιούμενοι." Besides, linking the second adverb to the following verse does not solve the issue since the present participle "μνημονεύοντες—remembering" in v.3 is part of the same sentence; (b) in Rom. 1:8-10 we have a similar example where the reason for thanksgiving is the faith of the Christians in Rome (compare I Thess. 1:3: "remembering your work of faith . . .") and where Paul describes his thanksgiving thus: "For God is my witness, whom I serve with my spirit in the gospel of his Son, that without ceasing—ἀδιαλείπτως—I mention you—μνείαν ὑμῶν ποιοῦμαι—always—πάντοτε—in my prayers—ἐπὶ τῶν

---

[16]We except I Thess. 1:2 since it is the subject of our discussion.

προσευχῶν μου" (Rom. 1:9-10; compare the literal parallelism of this text with I Thess. 1:2). We even find here that the two adverbs ἀδιαλείπτως and πάντοτε qualify one and same verb.[17]

4) Eph. 1:15-16 reads: "For this reason, because I have heard of your faith in the Lord Jesus and your love toward all the saints, I do not cease—οὐ παύομαι—to give thanks for you, remembering you in my prayers..." Here again, as in I Thess. 1:2-3, Paul gives thanks to God for what he heard about the faith and love of the Ephesians (compare I Thess. 1:3: "remembering your work of faith and labor of love..."), using the same expressions: εὐχαριστῶν, ὑπὲρ ἡμῶν,[18] μνείαν ποιούμενοι and ἐπὶ τῶν προσευχῶν μου (compare I Thess. 1:2). This shows that "I do not cease—οὐ παύομαι" is another way of rendering the idea of constancy. This conclusion is confirmed by the fact that οὐ παύομαι does not appear in Paul's letters except one other time,[19] and in an obvious reference to prayer: "... and (Epaphras) has made known to us your love in the Spirit. And so, from the day we heard of it, we have not ceased—οὐ παυόμεθα—to pray..." (Col. 1:8-9). Thus the use of οὐ παύομαι in a comparable way (i.e., in relation to prayer) to that of ἀδιαλείπτως is a clear proof that the idea of persistence and constancy in prayer is not a passing thought in the Apostle's mind, but is an essential aspect of the personality of Paul the believer. "Pray ceaselessly/constantly!" (I Thess. 5:17).

Prayer, especially in its thanksgiving form, is the pillar of the life of the true believer who knows that God is the source of every grace—χάρις—and that he owes Him thanks—εὐχαριστῶ. On the other hand, thanksgiving to God is but a part of the unceasing prayer life as it appears from the Apostle's statement: "in our prayers—ἐπὶ τῶν προσευχῶν

---

[17]We consider that the expression "always in my prayers—πάντοτε ἐπὶ τῶν προσεσχῶν μου" relates to what precedes rather than to what follows. The justification will be dealt with in our eventual commentary on Romans.

[18]In the first century A.D., writers did not differentiate between the propositions ὑπέρ and περί in their use with the genitive case. Thus ὑπὲρ ὑμῶν (Eph. 1:16) has the same meaning as περὶ ὑμῶν (I Thess. 1:2).

[19]We do not consider παύσονται in I Cor. 13:8 an exception to our statement for the following reasons: (a) the verb here is in the future tense; (b) it is not negated and thus its meaning is: (the tongues) will finish, cease, be done with; (c) it does not refer to the Apostle Paul, its subject being "γλῶσσαι—tongues."

ἡμῶν." And this means that Paul used to offer thanksgiving during his prayers, which in turn formed an essential
aspect of his life.

v.3. μνημονεύοντες ὑμῶν τοῦ ἔργου τῆς
πίστεως καὶ τοῦ κόπου τῆς ἀγάπης καὶ τῆς ὑπομονῆς τῆς ἐλπίδος
τοῦ κυρίου ἡμῶν Ἰησοῦ Χριστοῦ
ἔμπροσθεν τοῦ Θεοῦ καὶ πατρὸς
ἡμῶν,

remembering your work of faith and labor
of love and steadfastness of hope in our
Lord Jesus Christ before our God and Father;

The study of v.2 has shown us how Paul followed formally
the rules of contemporary letter writing, and yet he poured
into that old mould a totally new content. With v.3 we are
at the peak of this movement of transcending contemporary
usage: here we find that the reason for thanksgiving is neither
health nor strength nor wealth nor success, nor even the
multitude of gifts bestowed by God ... but it is that the
Christians in Thessalonica *believe, love* and *hope*. Thus in
the Apostle's eyes faith, love and hope are the qualities he
expects from each of the Christians of the churches he
founded, and this will remain his habit throughout his entire
life (see Rom. 1:8, Eph. 1:15; Phil. 1:9; Col. 1:8-9; II
Thess. 1:3; Philem. 4-5).

It is gratifying to note here that Paul's interest in this
triad of virtues is not the result of personal theological
thinking, as it might appear *prima facie*, but is rooted in

the tradition of the early church, where our Apostle had for a long time[20] breathed the air of living faith and orthodox teaching before he embarked with Barnabas on his missionary journeys.

We base this our statement on the following points:

1) It is well known that whenever Paul is expressing an idea special to him, he takes his time explaining and commenting in order to justify his stand. But when he brings up a point well established in the teaching of the early church he acts differently: he seems to be mentioning something from memory that comes spontaneously to his lips and that does not require further comment or explanation for the sake of the addressees, since they too are considered to be aware of the matter. Such is the case with our triad of virtues, as we shall endeavor to show.

2) At the outset of his first letter where he reminds the Thessalonians of the faith with which they have received the Gospel brought to them by him and his coadjutants (I Thess. 1:4-10), Paul mentions love and hope along with faith (v.3), even though there is no link between these two virtues and the subject matter. Such is also the case in Gal. 5:5-6 where, in the middle of his talk about a *faith* which *hopes* for righteousness, *i.e.*, the faith in Jesus Christ where there is no value to either circumcision or uncircumcision, the Apostle suddenly says: "For in Christ Jesus neither circumcision nor uncircumcision is of any avail, but *faith working through love*" (Gal. 5:6).

3) The same triad appears also at the outset of two other epistles: II Thess. 1:3-4 and Col. 1:4-5, where the subject matter is the behavior of the faithful. In Eph. 4 where the topic is also the behavior of the Christians, the triad appears again (vv.2, 4, 5).

4) In the two epistles to Timothy where the author admonishes his beloved disciple as to what virtues are incumbent upon a bishop, he comes to mention faith, love and steadfastness[21] in a sequence (I Tim. 6:11, II Tim. 3:10). In the epistle to Titus (which is also a pastoral letter) the same triad of faith, love and steadfastness appears not only in a row, but also all related to one and same present participle: "Bid the older men be temperate, serious, sensible,

---

[20]See Gal. 1:17-18, 21; Acts 9:30; 11:26.
[21]Regarding the similarity in meaning between hope and steadfastness, see below our comments on "your steadfastness of hope."

*sound in faith, in love and in steadfastness—*ὑγιαίνοντας τῇ πίστει,
τῇ ἀγάπῃ, τῇ ὑπομονῇ" (Tit. 2:2).

5) In I Thess. 5:8, Paul quotes the prophet Isaiah: "He put on
righteousness as a breastplate, and a helmet of salvation upon his
head" (Is. 59:17). It would have been logical for him to apply
only one virtue each to breastplate and the helmet; yet we read in
the above mentioned passage, "But, since we belong to the day, let
us be sober, and put on the breastplate of *faith and love*, and for
a helmet the *hope* of salvation." This inconsistency in dividing the
virtues between breastplate and helmet is due to the fact that at the
mention of faith the two other virtues came spontaneously to mind.
Or when Paul wanted to assign one virtue to each of the warfare
apparel, the three virtues rushed, as it were, in one block into his
imagination. Still the important thing is that, in either case, the one
explanation is that the unity between these virtues was common in
the early church teaching and that it was more powerful in the
Apostle's mind than the literary parallelism.

6) In the first letter to the Corinthians we find the ultimate proof
for our thesis. During his long digression on love (chap. 13) Paul
suddenly says: "So faith, hope and love abide, these three" (v.13).
The intimate relationship between these three virtues results from
the following: (a) the sudden, quite abrupt reference to faith and
hope in a context specifically and lengthily dealing with love;
(b) the mention of the three virtues in a row was done so quickly
that the author forgot the inclusion of the definite article ἡ before
each of them, so that the Greek text sounds like this: "as for now
remains faith, hope, love, these three"; (c) the verb "abide/ remain—
μένει" is in the singular although the plural "μένουσι" is expected.[22]
It is as if the Apostle were speaking of one reality that summarizes
the situation of the faithful "now—νυνί," in this life; (d) lastly—
and this is the most important consideration—the inclusion of "these
three—τὰ τρία ταῦτα" immediately after the mention of the triad
of virtues and without any further comment, confirms that "these"
were common knowledge among the faithful of the early church
and that they were "three."

7) A thorough study of the New Testament will confirm that

---

[22]In Greek a verb may be used in the third person singular with a subject
in the plural only if the subject is neuter, whereas πίστις—faith, ἐλπίς—
hope and ἀγάπη—love are all feminine. Now, if we consider that the
verb μένει refers to the words "τὰ τρία ταῦτα—these three" (which are
in the neuter) we shall arrive at the same conclusion, namely that these
virtues are linked together and form one reality (see the point 6d).

the unity of those three virtues was widespread in the essential
teaching of the first-century church, since we find the same triad
in other writings: Heb. 6:10-12; 10:22-23; I Pet. 1:5-7; Rev.
2:19.

Thus, at the occasion of thanksgiving during his constant
prayers Paul mentioned with liveliness those for whom he
was praying. To be sure, he remembered that they lived at
the level of that triad of virtues which became the pillar
of Christian teaching and life among the faithful of the
apostolic church. Yet our Apostle was not satisfied with the
mere mention of these virtues as if they were abstract, eso-
teric, having to do with our innermost feelings, impossible
to talk about, only between God and the individual, without
reference to our responsibility towards our brethren. As for
Paul, he made it clear that he used to remember in his
prayers the actual works resulting from those virtues, in
other words he remembered the virtues in their daily living
expression which is subject to anyone willing to check on
the reality of those virtues.

It is thus clear that Paul remembered not the faith of the
Thessalonians but the work—ἔργον—of that faith; and the
Greek word ἔργον actually means the action resulting from
work. It is then insufficient to repeat with him: "yet we
who know that a man is not justified by works of the law
but through faith in Jesus Christ, even we have believed in
Christ Jesus, in order to be justified by faith in Christ, and
not by works of the law, because by works of the law shall
no one be justified" (Gal. 2:16; see also Rom. 3:20, 28;
4:5; 11:5-6 and generally the whole of the epistle to the
Romans), since the Apostle is speaking here of the works
of the law which the Jews in general, and the Pharisees in
particular, used to boast about implementing, believing that
man was justified by that. Paul himself says elsewhere: "For
by grace you have been saved through faith; and this is not
your own doing, it is the first gift of God *not because of
works*, lest any man should boast. For we are his workman-

ship, *created* in Christ Jesus *for good works,* which God
prepared beforehand, *that we should walk in them"* (Eph.
2:8-10).

It clearly results that, in Paul's eyes, true faith—faith that
justifies—is bound to be expressed through specific actions.
"Thus you will know them by their fruits!" (Mt. 7:20).
That explains some bewildering Pauline statements such as:
"because we *have heard of your faith* in Christ Jesus and of
the love which you have for all the saints" (Col. 1:4; see also
Philem. 5); "For though I am absent in body, yet I am with
you in spirit, rejoicing *to see* your good order and *the firmness of your faith* in Christ" (Col. 2:5); "First, I thank
my God through Jesus Christ for all of you, because *your
faith is proclaimed* in all the world" (Rom. 1:8). How
could faith be seen, heard or proclaimed unless it becomes
actions that shine in the surrounding world? If our faith
is not active, then in vain is our hope in being justified, according to Paul himself: "For through the Spirit by faith,
we wait for the hope of righteousness. For in Christ Jesus
neither circumcision nor uncircumcision is of any avail, but
faith working through love—πίστις δι᾽ ἀγάπης ἐνεργου-
μένη" (Gal. 5:5-6).

Regarding love, the Apostle qualifies it with labor, or
more specifically tiring endeavor or hard and tiring work,
as the word κόπος actually means. This Greek expression
usually denotes manual labor. This is what appears from
the New Testament use of either the noun κόπος or the
related verb κοπιάω (Lk. 5:5; Jn. 4:38; Acts 20:34-35;
Rom. 16:6; I Cor. 3:8; 4:12; II Cor. 6:5; Eph. 4:28; II Tim.
2:6). Let us note here in particular three Pauline texts, namely
II Cor. 11:27, I Thess. 2:9, II Tim. 3:8, where κόπος is
mentioned along with μόχθος which means exhausting work
or overwhelming endeavor. All this means that in the
Apostle's mind, true love cannot be understood except when
it flows out as a continual endeavor in the service of others
(see Eph. 1:15; Col. 1:4; II Thess. 1:3; Philem. 5). This

also means that Christian love is physically tiring and exhausting, since the man is a whole and if he serves, then he
does so also with his hands and feet and not only with his
heart and feelings. Whenever we read that Paul remembers
in his prayers the love of the faithful, we must understand
that what was impressed into his memory was rather the
fruit of such love: the overwhelming, tiring and exhausting
endeavor.

Lastly, Paul remembers in his prayers the steadfastness/
patience in hope of the Thessalonians. The Lord has said:
"But he who endures to the end will be saved" (Mt. 10:22;
24:13; Mk. 13:13). And here the Apostle repeats after him
that steadfastness is the most important aspect of a life of
hope. Indeed, if we examine his epistles to the churches we
shall find that the notion of patience is somehow a definition of, another expression for hope. Thus seven times out
of a total of thirteen instances where the word "steadfastness/
patience/endurance—ὑπομονή" appears, we find it immediately linked to either "hope—ἐλπίς" or the verb "to
hope—ἐλπίζω" (Rom. 5:2-5/twice; 8:25; 15:4-5/twice; II
Cor. 1:6-10; I Thess. 1:3). Also the verb "to endure, be stead-
fast, be patient—ὑπομένω" is mentioned twice in these
epistles; once with the noun ἐλπίς (Rom. 12:12) and the
other time with the verb ἐλπίζω (I Cor. 13:7). On the
other hand, we find that whenever the word "patience—ὑπομονή" appears along with faith and love, the Apostle does
not feel the need of including hope: II Thess. 1:3-4; I Tim.
6:11; II Tim. 3:10; Tit. 2:2. The same is quite interestingly
found in II Pet. 1:5-7 as well as Rev. 2:10. All the above
points towards the fact that in the early church steadfastness/
patience became the most suitable and correct expression for
hope to the extent that, quite often, it simply took its place in
the mind of the Christians. This is then what the early
church lived by and the New Testament reflects, namely
that hope and steadfastness are two faces of the same reality: the former stretches forward in expectation of the

Lord's coming, while the latter implants the faithful at the
heart of daily life. This is reflected in the vitality of Paul's
prayer; he looked at or remembered the works, labor and
steadfastness of the Thessalonians, and rejoiced before the
Lord about their faith, love and hope, those three!

In v.3. the exegete is confronted with two syntactical difficulties. The first
one comes from the fact that, in the Greek text, the set of words: work of
faith, labor of love and steadfastness of hope, are preceded by the genitive
"ὑμῶν—your" and followed by the genitive "τοῦ κυρίου ἡμῶν Ἰησοῦ
Χριστοῦ—of our Lord Jesus Christ." It is obvious that ὑμῶν refers to the
three sets of words. The question remains whether the genitive τοῦ κυρίου
ἡμῶν Ἰησοῦ Χριστοῦ is complement to the three sets or only to the
last word "ἐλπίδος—hope"? If one opts for the first position, then the
meaning will be "remembering before our God and Father your work of
faith and labor of love and steadfastness of hope, these all being the result
of the work of the Lord Jesus Christ in you," and ensuing difficulties are
avoided.

If the choice is made for the alternative, namely that "the hope is in
our Lord Jesus Christ," then the difficulty arises as to whether the expression at the end of the verse in Greek "ἔμπροσθεν τοῦ Θεοῦ καὶ
πατρὸς ἡμῶν—before our God and Father" is to be taken with "μνημονεύοντες—remembering" at the beginning of the verse, or should follow
in meaning "ἐλπίδος τοῦ κυρίου ἡμῶν Ἰησοῦ Χριστοῦ—hope (which
is) in our Lord Jesus Christ"?

Our conviction is that the most accurate translation is: "remembering
your work of faith and labor of love and steadfastness of (the) hope (which
is/you have) in the Lord Jesus Christ before our God and Father." The
intended meaning here is that hope awaits the coming of the Lord Jesus at
the end of days as well as salvation in His name when we shall stand before
the throne of God the Father at the last judgment. Following are the reasons
for this our interpretation:

1) In his letters Paul never uses two subjective genitives to the same
word or words without the conjunction "καί—and."

2) The preposition "ἔμπροσθεν—before" is found only seven times in
Paul's writings, in five of which it is in relation with either God the Father
or Jesus Christ:[23] II Cor. 5:10; I Thess. 1:3; 2:19; 3:9, 13. In three
instances (II Cor. 5:10; I Thess. 2:19; 3:13) it is obvious that the topic
is the second coming of the Lord and the last judgment. As for I Thess.
3:9, it reads thus: "For what thanksgiving can we render to God for you,
for all the joy which we feel for your sake before—ἔμπροσθεν—our God."
Here also intended is that ultimate joy that will fill up the Apostle's heart
when he stands before the seat of God to be judged for his deeds (see our
comment on this verse further).

---

[23]The two other instances are: "...I said to Cephas before them all—
ἔμπροσθεν πάντων" (Gal. 2:14), and "...forgetting what lies behind
and straining forward to what lies ahead—τοῖς δὲ ἔμπροσθεν" (Phil.
3:13). It is only obvious that they do not concern us here.

3) The preposition ἔμπροσθεν appears four times in the first three chapters of our epistle, in three of which the reference is to standing before God at the last judgment. Further, these chapters form an organic unit, in that in them Paul reminds his readers of specific historical events related to their acceptance of the faith as a result of his preaching, and that he is trying his best to keep them in that faith.

4) In I Thess. 2:19; 3:9, 13 we see that the mention of the last judgment is related to the Apostle's fear that the Thessalonians' faith might have faltered, and consequently that his preaching might have failed.[24] In our text too it appears from vv.4-8 that the main point in Paul's mind is the gospel message he brought to them on the one hand (v.5), and their faith on the other (vv.6-8).

As for the virtue of hope, its ultimate pole of attraction— one might even say its reason for being—is the Lord Jesus Christ, since He alone is able to save us from the coming wrath (see v.10) when we shall stand before the judgment seat of God. And the reason is that, in Christ, God is our Father. That is why the Apostle says that at the day of judgment we shall be standing "before our God and *Father.*" If patience sometimes seems to be the key to some kind of human solution, salvation at the last day will only be the result of a perseverance until the end, as the Lord Himself puts it (Mt. 10:22; 24:13; Mk. 13:13). But such a stead-fastness is impossible unless it stems out of hope in the Lord Jesus Christ, *i.e.,* a hope roted in the person of Jesus who redeemed us on the cross and rose from the dead to save us from the wrath of the last day. Let us then put our hope in Him alone, forbearing difficulties and afflictions in total joy (v.6), proclaiming our faith in God to the whole world (v.8) and sacrificing ourselves in every kind of labor proceeding from an infinite love towards the others (v.3)!

---

[24]The importance of this point in Paul's eyes has to do with his belief that he will ultimately be judged on the basis of his apostleship, *i.e.,* on the basis of whether he will have succeeded or not in his apostolic ministry (see Phil. 2:16; 4:1; I Thess. 2:19; II Thess. 1:4-5).

v.4. εἰδότες, ἀδελφοί, ἠγαπημένοι ὑπὸ Θεοῦ, τὴν ἐκλογὴν ὑμῶν,

For we know, brethren beloved by God, that you are chosen;

The word "brethren—ἀδελφοί" does not need any comment since even someone reading the New Testament for the first time will realize that in the early church this expression became the name by which the faithful were known. Hence the tradition in our church according to which the reader of the epistle in the liturgical service begins the assigned reading by saying "Brethren"[25] even when this word is not part of the text. Such a tradition does not introduce any addition to the inspired text, since in all the epistles (Pauline and others—with the exception of Titus and Jude) the word "brethren—ἀδελφοί" appears to indicate the Christians. That usage is obviously related to our being children of God the Father, acquired through the Lord Jesus Christ, in that the Spirit of the Son cries in us: "Abba—Father" (see the explanation of v.1 above). This, our being God's children, is also reflected in Paul's words about the faithful: "For those whom He foreknew He also predestined to be conformed to the image of *His Son,* in order that He might be the *firstborn among many brethren*" (Rom. 8:29). The brotherhood of Christians in the church is thus an outcome of their childhood to God which took place in Jesus Christ and which creates the similarity between them. That is precisely what makes it different from the idea of brotherhood in its human acceptance, which is rooted in different kinds of bonds: familial, tribal, national, partisan, political, economic, *etc.*

---

[25]We except the pastoral epistles (I Tim., II Tim., Tit.) for they are addressed to individuals. Thus, the word "brethren" gives way to either "My son Timothy" or "My son Titus."

This is why the Apostle hurries, after his first use of this expression, to qualify that the Thessalonian faithful are brethren because they *have been and still are beloved* by God. For this is actually the meaning of ἠγαπημένοι which is the perfect participle of the verb "to love—ἀγαπάω." It is well known that the perfect tense in Greek indicates a past event whose effect reaches into the present moment. We see two reasons for the importance of the word "beloved—ἠγαπημένοι":

1) It appears from the gospels that, in the two instances where He introduced Jesus Christ to the people, God said: "This is my beloved—ὁ ἀγαπητός—Son" (Mt. 3:17; Mk. 1:11; Lk. 3:22; Mt. 17:5; Mk. 9:7), which shows that Christ's Sonship to God the Father is a relationship of love. Hence John's repetition in his gospel that the Lord Jesus underlined in his teaching the Father's love for him: 3:35; 10:17; 15:9, 10; 17:23-24, 26. This means that our childhood towards God is also a relationship of love and that our brotherhood, as we mentioned above, is the result of God's love for us.[26]

2) The use of the perfect tense underlines that on the one hand God's love started at a specific point in time past, while on the other it is still effective today: (a) the point at which God's extreme love for the faithful of Thessalonica materialized was the moment of their chosenness (v.4), *i.e.*, their listening to (v.5) and acceptance/reception of (v.6) the Good News (see the explanation of vv.5 and 6); (b) the ongoing love of God for them is the basis of their ongoing brotherhood in Christ.

Moreover, Paul speaks in this verse about the "choice" of the faithful in Thessalonica. On purely linguistic terms the expression "τὴν ἐκλογὴν ὑμῶν—your choice" may mean either that the Thessalonians have chosen God or that God chose them. A quick glance at the other six instances where

---

[26]See Rom. 8:29-32, 35, 39.

ἐκλογή is found (Acts 9:15; Rom. 9:11; 11:5, 7, 28; II Pet. 1:10), as well as at the verses where the verb "ἐκλέγομαι—choose" or the adjective "ἐκλεκτός—chosen" appear, will show that the meaning is always that God chooses.

But the expression ἐκλογή carries another teaching which is extremely important to our Christian faith. This word does not appear in the Septuagint, which is an indication that it is proper to the early church. This, however, does not entail that the meaning is completely new, since the Septuagint uses profusely the verb ἐκλέγω and the adjective ἐκλεκτός, and it is well known that the concept of chosenness is central to the Old Testament. Still we will have to study the use of the noun ἐκλογή in the New Testament in order to grasp its precise meaning.

As we mentioned above, ἐκλογή appears only seven times in all the New Testament, five of which at Paul's hand. Now, since its use in Acts 9:15 has a special context, and since the writer of II Pet. knew very well all of Paul's letters (II Pet. 3:15-16) and thus was influenced by them, it is only but logical to limit our study to the use of ἐκλογή in the *corpus Paulinum*. Our work will be facilitated by the fact that four out of the five instances are found in one single unit in the epistle to the Romans (chap. 9-11). From the texts Rom. 9:11; 11:5, 28, it clearly appears that the meaning of ἐκλογή is that God's choice is not a result of works man does and which make him worthy of God's choice of him (9:11; 11:28), but that it is a grace and thus a gift of God (11:5-6). Now that which Paul calls *"remnant*[27] chosen by grace" in 11:5, he identifies as ἐκλογή in 11:7, which shows that ἐκλογή of v.7 has the meaning of "chosen or elect ones," and this is how it is rendered in all translations.

Our conclusion is that in Paul's mind the word ἐκλογή means: on the one hand God's act of choosing, and on the

---

[27]See Isaiah 4:3.

other the result of such a choice, *i.e.*, "the chosen remnant of Israel" (Rom. 11:5, 7). "What then? Israel failed to obtain what is sought. The elect/chosen—ἡ δὲ ἐκλογή—obtained it, but the rest were hardened" (v.7). This indicates that in I Thess. 1:4 the Apostle meant that the Thessalonians of heathen origin (1:9) had become chosen/elect, *i.e.*, part of the "chosen remnant of Israel," and that happened—as we shall see in vv.5 and 6—on the basis of their acceptance of Paul's, Silvanus' and Timothy's preaching to them. The Gospel and the news of salvation which it carries is then that which makes out of the believing heathens "brethren," "God's beloved children," "members of the chosen remnant of Israel" without their entering into membership in the Jewish people. That is the radical change that took place at "the fullness of time" (Gal. 4:4), namely: God realized His purpose/plan (Rom. 9:11) in the proclamation of His love to every man in Jesus Christ, thus making out of every human being one of His elect. Here we come to the same conclusion which we attained through study of the expression "the church of the Thessalonians" in v.1. And the Apostle states that he and his companions "know—εἰδότες" all that because they remember what happened in Thessalonica when they brought the gospel message there.

v.5. ὅτι τὸ εὐαγγέλιον ἡμῶν οὐκ ἐγενήθη εἰς ὑμᾶς ἐν λόγῳ μόνον ἀλλὰ
καὶ ἐν δυνάμει καὶ ἐν πνεύματι
ἁγίῳ καὶ πληροφορίᾳ πολλῇ, καθὼς οἴδατε οἷοι ἐγενήθημεν ἐν ὑμῖν
δι᾽ ὑμᾶς.

for our gospel came to you not only in word,

but also in power and in the Holy Spirit and
with much/complete fullness. You know what
kind of men we proved to be among you for
your sake.

In the first century A.D. the conjunction ὅτι was not only
causal, having the meaning "because." It also was used to
explain or confirm the previous statement and thus meant
"since, on the basis that, in that." We believe that here ὅτι
has the latter sense for the following reasons: (a) in his
letters the Apostle never tries to prove to his addressees the
truthfulness of their election. This has never presented itself
as an issue in the minds of the faithful; (b) the present
participle "εἰδότες—knowing" of v.4 has the connotation
of remembrance and does not reflect any epistemological
process; (c) in vv.5-10 Paul simply states the facts which
clearly show not only *how* the Thessalonians became chosen
(v.5), but also the fruits of such an election: their for-
bearance of affliction joyfully (v.6) and their faith that
became a living example for all faithful (v.7).

In relating the way in which the Thessalonians were
chosen by God, Paul starts by mentioning the immediate
cause of that great event in the lives of some of that city's
inhabitants, namely: the gospel—τὸ εὐαγγέλιον. We have
become accustomed to understanding by this word the first
four books of the New Testament: Matthew, Mark, Luke
and John. In fact the practice of thus naming these books
did not start until the second century, whereas the word
εὐαγγέλιον appears no less than fifty times in Paul's letters, which were mostly written before the appearance of the
first gospel and thus independently from it. This situation
justifies the following digression, which attempts to clarify
the meaning of that extremely important word in the early
church's theological vocabulary.

The ancient Greeks called εὐαγγέλιον the amount of money given to the bringer of good news. With time the same word began to be used for the good news itself, and that was the situation in the first century A.D. The church, which naturally borrowed from the contemporary general vocabulary, used the same word to denote the Gospel, *i.e.*, the ultimate Good News which brings to the whole world the tidings of its salvation in Jesus Christ from sin and death that suffocated it. This is confirmed by Paul's use of this word in his epistles.

However, a full study of the Pauline literature brings us to the conclusion that the Apostle used that word in four different ways:[28] (a) the gospel of God (I Thess. 2:2, 8, 9); (b) the gospel of Jesus Christ (I Thess. 3:2; II Thess. 1:8); (c) our gospel (I Thess. 1:5; 2:14) or my gospel (Rom. 2:16; 16:25); (d) the gospel (I Thess. 2:4).

The gospel is God's because He is the author of the Good News and the One who promised it through His prophets in the Holy Scriptures (Rom. 1:1-2). It is Jesus Christ's gospel because He also is God and shares with the Father in every work, especially in the work of salvation, as it is clear from Paul's words: "For Christ did not send me to baptize but to preach the gospel— εὐαγγελίζεσθαι" (I Cor. 1:17). But the gospel is Christ's in yet another more profound and more important meaning, namely: the content of the Good News is Jesus Christ Himself in His saving death and resurrection (Rom. 1:3-4; I Cor. 4:15 and especially 15:1-7). Yet the Apostle does not limit himself to the two afore-mentioned expressions, but more than once bluntly qualifies the gospel as being his own: my/own gospel. This shows how much the preacher is, practically speaking, an integral part of the gospel he carries, and how it becomes defined by him as much as it is by either its author or its content. However, the preacher's sharing in the gospel happens in fact in his action of preaching, *i.e.*, the gospel is his insofar as he carries it to the others. Thus the expression "my gospel" may indicate either the content of the Good News, *i.e.*, *the gospel I carry*, or the act of preaching, *i.e.*, *that I carry it*, or even both. The interpreter will have to clarify in each case which

---

[28]We mention only the instances found in the two epistles to the Thessalonians to save space.

meaning the expression "my/our gospel" has, or whether it carries
simultaneously both meanings. As for the absolute "the gospel,"
it bears all three previous meanings.

In our passage the expression "our gospel—τὸ εὐαγγέλιον ἡμῶν" renders the idea of the preaching activity Paul
and his companions exercised among the Thessalonians rather
than the Good News they brought. Indeed: (a) the Apostle
underlines that his gospel did not take place in word only,
but also with the action of the Holy Spirit, and this would
apply only to the missionary activity he had among them
(see also I Cor. 2:4-5); (b) Paul says that his gospel took
place/happened to—εἰς—the Thessalonians. Now, the preposition εἰς indicates direction; it is as if the gospel *came to*
the inhabitants of that city; (c) at the end of the verse
Paul reminds his readers "how we were—οἷοι ἐγενήθημεν,"
i.e., "how we behaved," among/towards you; (d) a little
further on, still speaking on the same topic, the Apostle twice
uses the expression "our coming/entrance to/towards you—
εἴσοδον ἡμῶν πρὸς ὑμᾶς" (1:9; 2:1), which indicates
the arrival of our missionaries in Thessalonica and their
activity there.

Now this activity "happened not only in word, but also
in power and in the Holy Spirit and with much/complete
fullness." Here we find for the first time[29] on Paul's lips
the statement that his preaching was not only in words, but
that God bestowed on him that which could back his sayings,
give them power and confirm their truth before his listeners.
And this gift of God was rendered by the Apostle with the
following expressions: power—δύναμις, Holy Spirit—πνεῦμα ἅγιον, and much/complete fullness—πληροφορία
πολλή. Yet we may not, in such a detailed commentary,
satisfy ourselves with the enumeration of such words without

---

[29]The Apostle will come back to this important point in I Cor. 2:1-5 and
Rom. 15:18-19.

trying our best to shed on them as much light as possible, with the hope of bringing out their actual meaning.

We shall start our research with the first two expressions, leaving until later the study of πληροφορία, for two reasons: (a) this word appears only four times in the whole New Testament; (b) in our text it is linked to the expression "Holy Spirit," as we will show later.

In the Pauline writings, δύναμις appears always (except for Rom. 15:13, 19; I Cor. 2:4; I Thess. 1:5) along with God and it indicates, as in the Old Testament, His effectiveness in the domain of creation, His acting and effective power in our world, *i.e.*, it indicates God in His coming to us and in His realizing within and around us His plan of salvation. And this is quite clear in that whenever δύναμις appears, the subject is always the salvation wrought by God.

As for the Holy Spirit, He always appears in the role of the one realizing and actualizing in the faithful the result of God's salvation: He pours in us God's love (Rom. 5:5), He shouts in us the cry of our sonship to God (Rom. 8:14-16; Gal. 4:6) and thus assures us of being heirs (Gal. 4:7; Eph. 1:13-14), He makes grow in us the fruits of God's kingdom (Rom. 14:17; Gal. 5:21-22), He makes us spell out the true faith (I Cor. 12:3), He distributes among us the gifts that edify the body of Christ (I Cor. 12:4-14), in Him was manifested the mystery of Christ that had been hidden for ages (Eph. 3:4-6, 9).

The conclusion from all the above is that the Holy Spirit is the actual/factual bearer of God's power. It is thus necessary to study now the four passages in which the two expressions appear together, namely: Rom. 15:13, 19; I Cor. 2:4 and I Thess. 1:5. Of special importance for us are the last three because they are very similar not only in the use of the expressions together, but also in that: (a) they all speak of the gospel carried or brought by Paul (Rom. 15:19; I Cor. 2:1, 4; I Thess. 1:5); (b) they all stress that his preaching was not only in word (Rom. 15:19; I Cor. 2:1, 4;

I Thess. 1:5); (c) the backing for the Apostle's words was
"in power and in the Holy Spirit" (I Thess. 1:5), "in
demonstration of the Spirit and of power" (I Cor. 2:4), "in
the power of signs and wonders, by the power of the Holy
Spirit" (Rom. 15:19).

From I Cor. 2:4 it results that Paul's preaching did not
use the power of conviction based on human wisdom, but on
a proof from the Holy Spirit acting with God's power. And
the appearance of the word "ἀπόδειξις—demonstration/
proof" in a letter addressed to people in whose ranks were
circulating accusations against the Apostle, shows that Paul
was using it in all sobriety and seriousness, and that his
intention was the following: the ultimate proof for the correctness of his teaching was an action done in power by
the Holy Spirit, a clear and apparent action that defies any
discussion or denial on the part of the Corinthian Christians . . . otherwise how could it still be a proof? Anyway,
we do know from his second letter to the same Corinthians—which was written following the broadcasting of
the accusations against his apostleship—that he felt forced
(II Cor. 12:11) to take up a bitter action of self-defense he
had never wished (12:11), calling it foolishness (12:11),
and at this occasion he writes, "the signs of a true apostle
were performed among you in all patience, *with signs and
wonders and mighty works/powers*—σημείοις τε καὶ τέ-
ρασιν καὶ δυνάμεσιν. For in what were you less favored
than the rest of the churches, except that I myself did not
burden you?" (II Cor. 12:12-13); which means that the ultimate tangible proof of Paul's true apostleship was—besides
his extreme patience—the signs, wonders and mighty works
which took place at his hands.

The same idea comes back in another passage where Paul
speaks of his missionary activity: ". . . For I will not venture
to speak of anything except what Christ has wrought through
me to win obedience from the Gentiles, by word and deed—
λόγῳ καὶ ἔργῳ, by the power of signs and wonders, by

the power of the Spirit—ἐν δυνάμει σημείων καὶ τερά-
των, ἐν δυνάμει πνεύματος—so that from Jerusalem and
as far round as Illyricum[30] I have fully preached the gospel
of Christ" (Rom. 15:18-19). Here also we find the Apostle
of the Gentiles performing his duty not only in word but
also in deed, meaning the signs and wonders. Now the
obvious parallelism in v.19: by the power of signs and
wonders/by the power of the Spirit (and the meaning here
is by the power of signs and wonders, that is by the power
of the Spirit), shows beyond doubt that the signs and wonders
are the work of the Holy Spirit.

Our research has brought us to two new words: σημεῖον,
plural σημεῖα (sign); and τέρας, plural τέρατα (miracle/
wonder). The important point in all this is that τέρας
appears only sixteen times in the New Testament, always in
the plural τέρατα and always together with σημεῖον,
again under the plural form σημεῖα.[31] In all these passages
without exception (see especially Jn. 4:48; Acts 2:22, 43;
4:30; 5:12; 6:8; 7:36; Heb. 2:4) the meaning is obvious,
namely: the miracles and wonders.

Let us try here to answer a question that might come to the
reader's mind: What about the use of δύναμις in its plural form
δυνάμεις? The answer is simple. In such cases the noun used
in the singular to express a certain action is used in the plural to
indicate the outcome/result of such an action, like speaking of God's
mercy on the one hand and about the mercies resulting from it on
the other hand. This explains the use of δύναμις in its plural
form δυνάμεις in the sense of miracles or wonders, especially in
the synoptic gospels.[32] Anyway, this meaning of δύναμις results from
the following considerations:

---

[30]A province of what was then the Roman Empire. It is geographically
situated in present-day Yugoslavia.

[31]Mt. 24:24; Mk. 13:22; Jn. 4:48; Acts 2:19, 22, 43; 4:30; 5:12; 6:8;
7:36; 14:3; 15:12; Rom. 15:19; II Cor. 12:12; II Thess. 2:9; Heb. 2:4.
In Acts 14:3 and 15:12 the subject matter is Paul and Barnabas during their
first missionary journey.

[32]The synoptic gospels are Mt., Mk., and Lk. "Synoptic" is from a
Greek word that means "seeing together, at the same time." It denotes the

1) In some instances δύναμις is used together with τέρατα and σημεῖα (Acts 2:22 and II Cor. 12:12).

2) In Acts 8:13 we read: "Even Simon himself believed, and after being baptized he continued with Philip. And seeing signs and great miracles—σημεῖα καὶ δυνάμεις μεγάλας—performed, he was amazed," where δυνάμεις takes the place of τέρατα.

3) While in Acts 14:3 and 15:12 we read that signs and wonders—σημεῖα καὶ τέρατα—happened at the hands of Paul and Barnabas, we find in Acts 19:11-12 the following text: "And God did extraordinary powers—δυνάμεις—by the hands of Paul so that handkerchiefs or aprons were carried away from his body to the sick, and diseases left them and the evil spirits came out of them."

We come thus to the following conclusion: in saying that his preaching in Thessalonica was not only in word but also in power and in the Holy Spirit, Paul means that he was granted to perform many miracles that confirmed the truth of his apostleship as well as the correctness of his gospel.

And now, what about the expression "and with much/complete fullness—καὶ πληροφορία πολλῇ" after "and in the Holy Spirit"? Πληροφορία appears extremely rarely in the New Testament: only four times,[33] whereas the verb πληροφορέω is not found more than six times;[34] hence the difficulty of pinpointing the exact meaning of this word. We do know that πληροφορέω means to bring to completion, to fill up, to complete, to perfect, and this sense fits the following passages: Lk. 1:1; Col. 2:2; 4:12; II Tim. 4:5, 17; Heb. 6:11; 10:22. In the remaining two verses (Rom. 4:12 and 14:5) the meaning seems rather to be mental realization, or full assuredness of something, or complete conviction. But this meaning itself bears the idea of arriving at a full assuredness resulting from a complete inner fullness. There-

---

fact that these three gospels are so similar that one can put their text in three parallel columns and view all of them at once. Now the fourth evangelist prefers the use of "σημεῖα—signs" when speaking of the Lord Jesus' miracles.

[33]Col. 2:2; I Thess. 1:5; Heb. 6:11; 10:22.

[34]Lk. 1:1; Rom. 4:21; 14:5; Col. 4:12; II Tim. 4:5, 17.

fore we preferred to translate here πληροφορία as fullness rather than realization or conviction, since this meaning fits better the present context. Thus the Apostle seems to be saying: "Our preaching out did not happen only in words, but also with the convincing power of miracles and wonders resulting from the action of the Holy Spirit. And that action was full to the utmost so that we might say that the Holy Spirit has poured out completely and fully his energy."

We may add here that πληροφορία in our text is directly linked to the expression "the Holy Spirit" through the conjunction "and— καί" without the repetition of the preposition "in—ἐν," so that the verse reads: "in power and in the Holy Spirit and complete fullness." Thus πληροφορία is linked in meaning to "the Holy Spirit." In other words, it is not parallel to the words "power" and "Holy Spirit,"[35] but is rather complementary to the latter and is to be understood with it.

The verb "you know—οἴδατε" does not appear in any other Pauline letter with the same frequency as in this letter: nine times in five chapters, out of which seven are in the first three chapters, that is once every six verses! And in all these instances the Thessalonians are invited to recall specific past events. If we add to our count "You remember—μνη-μονεύετε" in 2:9, "God is witness" in 2:5 and "You are witnesses, and God also" in 2:10, we arrive at the following conclusion: in this our epistle Paul quotes historical events almost once every four verses in the first three chapters. This indicates that the Apostle was facing in the church of Thessalonica a very delicate and dangerous situation that forced him to write a letter full of references to past events, as if this were the only way for him to convince the faithful there of the correctness of his statements. The gospel preaching is not an action taking place purely on the inner level of our lives; it is an historical event which is stamped in the memory of the people in a tremendously convincing way. We believe

---

[35]Anyhow such a combination is never found in Paul's letters.

that any gospel preaching that does not take this reality into consideration is bound to fail sooner or later. Feelings, emotions, and psychological excitement are for the divine word but a ground without depth, where the grass withers in the sun since it has no roots (Mk. 4:5). God's Word bears fruit only when sown in a good ground, in man's heart and mind and memory, *i.e.*, at the heart of his being.

Now, the expression "as you well know—καθὼς οἴδατε" in our verse seems to present some difficulty to the interpreter. The question is whether this expression depends on what precedes, *i.e.*, "for our gospel came/happened—ἐγενήθη—to you not only in word...," or pertains to what follows, *i.e.*, "what kind of men we proved to be—οἷοι ἐγενήθημεν—among you for your sake." To be able to come up with the correct answer we would have to consider the other passages where Paul uses καθὼς οἴδατε (2:2, 5; 3:4) or καθάπερ οἴδατε (2:11). In all these cases we shall find that our expression *follows* a given verb or present participle. In our view this would be enough to opt for the first alternative. However, such a stand would leave us with another difficulty regarding the latter part of v.5: "what kind of men we proved to be among you for your sake." That is why we consider the only solution to be that καθὼς οἴδατε refers to this phrase as well.

The following are the points that justify our opinion:

1) A heavy and complex syntax—such as the one resulting from our reading of v.5—is a common feature of Paul's letters, which often makes their translation difficult.

2) Paul used to dictate his epistles to one of his helper scribes. Therefore our guess is that the remotness of the verb ἐγενήθη in the phrase which he intended to confirm with καθὼς οἴδατε made him repeat immediately following this expression the same verb, but in another form, *viz.* the first person plural: ἐγενήθημεν.

3) Moreover, the expression καθὼς οἴδατε resp. καθάπερ οἴδατε, qualifies twice the verb ἐγενήθημεν in chap. 2 (vv.5 and 11). This indicates that by using it the Apostle is referring to the

way in which he appeared in Thessalonica. A further confirmation is found in the third use of καθὼς οἴδατε immediately after: "but though we had already suffered and been shamefully treated ..." (2:2).

4) The comparison of the Thessalonians to himself and his companions in v.6 is linked to the preceding verse by the conjunction "and—καί." Now the point of comparison here—as will appear from our comments on v.6—is that both parties have undergone with joy the great affliction caused by the gospel and have resumed their course. But this idea does not appear in the first part of v.5. That is what made Paul introduce it at the end of the verse to be a bridge to the following verse.

5) The proof that Paul's intention in saying "... what kind of men we proved to be among you for your sake" is that which we read in 2:2 regarding the affliction he suffered because of the gospel, results from the following points: (a) verses 6-10 of chapter one are nothing but a parenthesis about the Thessalonians' behavior towards Paul's gospel, in a passage where the Apostle's main intention is to speak of his preaching in their city (1:5 and 2:1-12); (b) the verb "you know—οἴδατε" disappears suddenly in 1:6-10 to come again twice in a row in 2:1-2; (c) the same verb "to be/to become/to appear—γίγνομαι" is used to reflect the Apostles' behavior (ἐγενήθημεν) as well as that of the faithful in Thessalonica (ἐγενήθητε); (d) the emphasis is on the fact that the Thessalonians were imitators of Paul and his companions.

Consequently, in order to render accurately Paul's intention, we would opt for the following interpretive translation of v.5: "For our gospel came to you not only in word, but also in power and in the Holy Spirit and with much fullness, as you well know. And you also know that we brought this gospel to you with joy in spite of the affliction which befell us previously in Philippi, and all that for your sake, *i.e.*, in order that we may secure you salvation through Jesus Christ." Such an interpretation is, in our eyes, the only one that keeps the logical sequence between verses 5 and 6.

Before moving to v.6 we consider it important to dwell a while upon the expression "for your sake—δι' ὑμᾶς." Its inclusion here shows that all that is mentioned in our verse—

Paul's sufferings first in Philippi and then in Thessalonica; the gospel which he brought them in words, *i.e.*, in preaching and guidance; the sharing of the Holy Spirit in the apostolic activity through miracles and wonders that brought about full conviction—happened for the Thessalonians' sake; all of it was in their service as if they were the masters over everything. This sheds light on Paul's understanding of apostleship. He sees in it an exhausting service to the others and considers himself a humble servant at their orders. Only if we become aware of this reality shall we understand what the Apostle of the Gentiles will write one day: "So let no one boast of men. For *all things are yours*, whether Paul or Apollos or Cephas or the world or life or death or the present or the future, *all are yours*; and you are Christ's, and Christ is God's . . . We are fools for Christ's sake, but you are wise in Christ. We are weak, but you are strong. You are held in honor, but we in disrepute. To the present hour we hunger and thirst, we are ill-clad and buffeted and homeless, and we labor working with our own hands. When reviled, we bless; when persecuted, we endure; when slandered, we try to conciliate; we have become, and are now, as the refuse of the world, the offscouring of all things" (I Cor. 3:21-23 and 4:10-13). May each of us understand that we may not boast except in the cross of our Lord Jesus Christ (Gal. 6:14), since "a disciple is not above his teacher" (Mt. 10:24). That is the price of the world's salvation!

v.6. καὶ ὑμεῖς μιμηταὶ ἡμῶν ἐγενήθητε καὶ τοῦ κυρίου, δεξάμενοι τὸν
λόγον ἐν θλίψει πολλῇ μετὰ χαρᾶς
πνεύματος ἁγίου,

And you became imitators of us and of the

Lord, for you received the word in much affliction, with joy of/inspired by the Holy
Spirit;

Starting with this verse, and until the end of chapter one,
Paul suddenly shifts to talk about the good result which
crowned his activity in Thessalonica, before going on to
finish his thoughts about the way in which he came to and
preached in that city. However, this shift loses its suddenness
if we accept, as we have argued above, that the passage "what
kind of men we proved to be among you for your sake" was
introduced due to the mention of great affliction in this
verse. And thus the text of chapter one becomes clear in its
intent. Paul is saying that the Thessalonians' chosenness (v.4)
happened at the gospel's reaching them (v.5) and at their
accepting it (v.6). Now this is so since the news of their
faith has gone forth to the surrounding areas (vv.7-8), namely
the news that they turned to the living God (v.9) and are
expecting the coming again of Jesus (v.10).

In our verse the Apostle reminds the faithful of Thessalonica that they became his imitators; but this might mean
that he is the ultimate reference for the life of the Christians
and the highest example to be emulated. Thus, in order to
dissipate any misunderstanding in their minds, Paul underlines that they imitated also the Lord, putting himself along
with them on the one and same level before the Lord Jesus.
With this he clarifies to them that their true pride lies in
their imitation of the Lord, as he will say at another occasion:
"Be imitators of me, as I am of Christ" (I Cor. 11:1).

But what is actually the point of comparison between the
Lord, Paul and the Thessalonians? We find the answer in
the second part of the verse: "for you received—δεξάμενοι—
the word in much affliction with joy inspired by the Holy
Spirit." The participle "δεξάμενοι—having received" is

explanatory and refers to the action on the Thessalonians'
part that made them imitators of Paul and the Lord. But it
is the latter who is the author of the word, while the
former is the one who preached it. Therefore, the only valid
common denominator among the three is nothing but the
great affliction that each of them underwent: the first in
his sowing the word on this earth—*i.e.*, the Lord, the second
in his carrying it to the world—*i.e.*, Paul, and the third in
their accepting it—*i.e.*, the faithful of Thessalonica. Moreover, the inclusion of the Lord's person in a passage about
imitation forces upon us the conclusion we arrived at in our
comments on v.5, *viz.*, in his saying, "what kind of men we
proved to be among you for your sake," the Apostle meant
the great affliction, namely the sufferings and shameful
treatments he had undergone in Philippi (2:2, see also Acts
16:19-24). Otherwise the addition "... and of the Lord" in
v.6 would be out of order.

This is very clear in the Greek text which reads: καὶ ὑμεῖς
μιμηταὶ ἡμῶν ἐγενήθητε καὶ τοῦ κυρίου. Its literal translation
would be: "And you, imitators of us you became, and also of the
Lord." It thus appears that the inclusion of "and also of the
Lord" after the verb "became"—which ends the idea mentioned before it—and not after "of us," is a clear-cut proof that the comparison
was meant first between the Thessalonians and Paul. As for the
Lord's person, it was mentioned because the point of comparison
applies *also* to Him.

The expression "the word—ὁ λόγος" in its absolute form,
i.e., without anything to define it, meant in the early church
vocabulary the Good News of the gospel. This clearly appears from a quick study of the use of this expression in
the New Testament. Thus, we read in the Book of Acts
about the preaching activity of Paul and his companions:
"Now those who were scattered because of the persecution
that arose over Stephen traveled as far as Phoenicia and
Cyprus and Antioch, speaking *the word* to none except

Jews" (11:19); "then they (*viz.* Paul and Barnabas) passed through Pisidia, and came to Pamphilia. And when they had spoken *the word* in Perga, they went down to Attalia" (14:24-25); "And they went through the region of Phrygia and Galatia, having been forbidden by the Holy Spirit to speak *the word* in Asia" (16:6). As regarding those who gathered around the apostles' preaching, we read: "But many of those who heard *the word* believed; and the number of the men came to about five thousand" (4:4); "While Peter was still saying this, the Holy Spirit fell on all who heard *the word*" (10:44); "Now these Jews were more noble than those in Thessalonica, for they received *the word* with all eagerness..." (17-11). In 8:4 we read in all clarity: "Now those who were scattered went about preaching (bringing the good news of) *the word*—εὐαγγελιζόμενοι τὸν λόγον." This is again confirmed in Peter's words: "Brethren, you know that in the early days God made choice among you, that by my mouth the Gentiles should hear *the word of the gospel*—τὸν λόγον τοῦ εὐαγγελίου—and believe" (15:7). Finally we mention here the reason given by the apostles for their inability to serve the tables and their asking the people to chose some ministers/deacons: "But we will devote ourselves to prayer and to the ministry of *the word*" (6:4). This reason is very much like the one given in I Cor. 1:14-17: "I am thankful that I baptized none of you except Crispus and Gaius; lest any one should say that you were baptized in my name. (I did baptize also the household of Stephanas. Beyond that, I do not know whether I baptized any one else.) For Christ did not send me to baptize but to preach—εὐαγγελίζεσθαι." At any rate, it is clear from I Thess. that Paul and his companions brought to Thessalonica the gospel—τὸ εὐαγγέλιον (v.5), whereas the faithful accepted the word—τὸν λόγον (v.6).

The word θλῖψις is from the verb θλίβω which means to press hard, to squeeze, to crush. Thus θλῖψις has the meaning of affliction or pressing distress; and it always in-

dicates physical or material rather than spiritual affliction,
as it clearly results from its use in the New Testament and
especially by Paul. At any rate it will appear from our epistle
that the affliction of both the Apostle (προπαθόντες, 2:2)
and the Thessalonians (ἐπάθετε, 2:14) reflects physical
sufferings, since the verb πάσχω (whence the forms προπαθόντες and ἐπάθετε) specifically indicates physical pain.

But the deep reason for Paul's complimenting the Thessalonians is that they bore that much affliction "with a joy
inspired by the Holy Spirit—μετὰ χαρᾶς πνεύματος
ἁγίου." It appears that their stand was so well known
that the Apostle used it as an example when addressing the
Corinthians: "We want you to know, brethren, about the
grace of God which has been shown in the churches of
Macedonia, for in a *severe test of affliction*, their *abundance
of joy* and their extreme poverty have overflowed in a wealth
of liberality on their part" (II Cor. 8:1-2). And as affliction
is an integral part not only of preaching the gospel, but also
of its acceptance (I Thess. 3:3-4), so also at the core of the
gospel stands joy, or rather joy in afflictions according to
Paul. "Now I rejoice in my sufferings for your sake..."
(Col. 1:24); "...With all our affliction, I am overjoyed"
(II Cor. 7:4). But which joy finds its noblest expression in
affliction except that joy which is the fruit of the Holy
Spirit (Gal. 5:22)? Indeed, it is not enough for this Spirit
to show His power in signs and wonders (I Thess. 1:5)—all
these are but an instrument towards the sublime aim—but
He realizes in the hearts of those who received Him the hope
of all creation: the Kingdom of God. Could it be otherwise
when "the Kingdom of God is...joy in the Holy Spirit"
(Rom. 14:17)? The true believer knows that God's kingship finds its way to the marrow of his bones, in his distress
and affliction for the gospel's sake, indeed in an overflowing
joy in the midst of distresses and afflictions; that this joy
stands as long as the Holy Spirit does...otherwise it is but
vanity of vanities! Paul knew it all too well when he shouted:

"Rejoice always" (I Thess. 5:16); "Rejoice in the Lord always; again I will say, rejoice" (Phil. 4:4).

v.7. ὥστε γενέσθαι ὑμᾶς τύπον πᾶσιν
τοῖς πιστεύσουσιν ἐν τῇ Μακεδονίᾳ
καὶ ἐν τῇ Ἀχαΐᾳ.

so that you became an example to all the believers in Macedonia and in Achaia.

The Apostle Paul was so impressed with the Thessalonians' joy in spite of their great affliction that he considered them an example to all the believers in Macedonia and Achaia. The importance of the effect which the behavior of those Christians had on Paul's mind is shown in that he used elsewhere the word "example—τύπον" only twice and in both cases of himself as a living example to be followed by his readers (II Thess. 3:9; Phil. 3:17; see also I Cor. 4:16; 11:1). As for the mention of Macedonia and Achaia, it is due to the fact that they were the two largest provinces in Greece and that Paul preached in them one after the other (see the Introduction).

The word "πιστεύουσιν—believers"—which is the present participle of the verb "πιστεύω—to believe"—became in the early church, along with "ἀδελφοί—brethren," a technical term for Christians. This is obvious to any reader of Acts and the Pauline epistles.[36]

---

[36]See Acts 2:44; 5:14; 13:39; Rom. 1:16; 3:22; 4:11; 10:4; I Cor. 1:21; Gal. 3:22; Eph. 1:19; I Thess. 1:7; 2:10, 13.

v.8. ἀφ᾽ ὑμῶν γὰρ ἐξήχηται ὁ λόγος
τοῦ κυρίου οὐ μόνον ἐν τῇ Μακεδονίᾳ καὶ ᾽Αχαΐᾳ, ἀλλ᾽ ἐν παντὶ τόπῳ
ἡ πίστις ὑμῶν ἡ πρὸς τὸν Θεὸν
ἐξελήλυθεν, ὥστε μὴ χρείαν ἔχειν
ἡμᾶς λαλεῖν τι·

For not only has the word of the Lord sounded
forth from you in Macedonia and Achaia, but
your faith in God has gone forth everywhere,
so that we need not say anything.

In this verse appears the expression "the word of the
Lord—ὁ λόγος τοῦ κυρίου" which also means the gospel.
This is clear enough from the Book of Acts which uses,
along with "the word," this our expression to indicate the
message of salvation brought by the apostles and their co-
workers. See Acts 8:25; 13:48-49; 15:36; 16:32; 19:10; and
especially 15:35 which reads: "But Paul and Barnabas remained in Antioch, teaching and preaching—εὐαγγελιζόμενοι—*the word of the Lord*, with many others also."

Consequently, the first question that comes to the reader's
mind is how to understand the first part of our verse. Does
the Apostle Paul mean that some of the Thessalonians went
on preaching the word of the Lord, *i.e.*, the gospel, in Macedonia and Achaia? The answer is definitely negative, and
that for the following considerations:

1) The conjunction "γάρ—for" at the beginning of our
verse indicates that the latter is explanatory of the previous
statement. Now the meaning of the two preceding verses is
that the Thessalonian Christians became, through their acceptance of the gospel in much affliction with joy inspired

by the Holy Spirit, an example to all the believers in Macedonia and Achaia.

2) We know that Paul was forced to leave Thessalonica (Acts 17:10), whence he brought the gospel to Athens (17:16-34) and then to Corinth (18:1-11), and that he wrote this letter upon his arrival in the capital of Achaia. It is thus quite improbable that the Thessalonians—concerning whom the Apostle was still worried (see the Introduction)—might have preceded him in evangelizing Macedonia, let alone Achaia.

3) Usually in Greek the expression "οὐ μόνον—not only" is followed by "ἀλλὰ καί—but also" (see v.5), whereas here we find simply "ἀλλά—but." Thus "ἀλλ' ἐν παντὶ τόπῳ—but in every place" cannot be understood with the preceding, but rather with the following: "your faith in God has gone forth everywhere."

Before trying to present our understanding of this verse, we would like to note here another point which, we believe, will help us to find the clue. A closer look at our verse 8 shows that it is a kind of parenthesis, since the flow of thought runs from v.7 to v.9. This results from the following: (a) v.8 does not give an immediate explanation to v.7, for in it we read how the news of their faith was spread to Macedonia and Achaia, but we find no comment on how they became an example to all the faithful there. The expected explanation to v.7 appears in vv.9-10, where we read that the faithful of Macedonia and Achaia are reporting—ἀπαγγέλλουσιν—how—πῶς—the Thessalonians became believers; (b) the personal pronoun "αὐτοί—these/they/themselves" in v.9 does not refer to any word in v.8, but to "τοῖς πιστεύουσιν—the believers" of v.7.

The question then is: if the logical explanation to v.7 is found in vv.9-10, what is the place of v.8? The only convincing answer seems to be that it shows us how the news about the Thessalonians' faith got to the Christians of Achaia and the rest of Macedonia, so that these in their turn were

telling about what had happened in Thessalonica (vv.9-10);
and in this way the faithful of this city had become an
example (v.7) to the brethren in other churches. Now, it is
only natural that such news would spread among Christian
communities, since only they would be interested in it as well
as able to report about it. But we know that the Christians
of Beroea (in Macedonia) and Achaia believed at the hands
of the Apostle, which means that the news of what took
place in Thessalonica arrived to them along with "the word
of the Lord" preached there by Paul and his companions.
In other words, the going forth of the Thessalonians' faith
means the spreading of the news about such a faith—and not
spreading of the faith either at their hands or through con-
tagion!—in that Paul carried along such news while preaching the gospel.

On the basis of the aforementioned we are confident in
saying that the most adequate meaning of v.8 is the following: "For from you—ἀφ' ὑμῶν (i.e., after having come
to you and stayed with you) the word of the Lord sounded
forth (i.e., my colleagues and I preached the gospel) in
Macedonia and Achaia; we have told there about what had
happened to us and you in Thessalonica (see v.9), and thus
your faith in God has gone forth (i.e., they learned of your
faith in God)."

There remains, however, one question: we know that this
our epistle was written during Paul's second missionary journey, i.e., that he (and the other apostles) had not yet completed their preaching; how must we then understand the
expression "but everywhere/in every place"? The first step
towards an answer should be a study of Paul's use of it. In
all his epistles addressed to the churches "ἐν παντὶ τόπῳ—
in every place" appears only three times (I Cor. 1:2; II Cor.
2:14; I Thess. 1:8). Now, in the first two instances the
meaning is obviously *every place reached by Paul's missionary
activity.*

Thus II Cor. 2:14 reads: "But thanks be to God, who in Christ always leads us in triumph, and *through us*—δι' ἡμᾶς—spreads the fragrance of the knowledge of him in every place." On the other hand, it appears from I Cor. 1:2[37] that the Apostle uses "ἐν παντὶ τόπῳ—in every place" to indicate specific places in a given province, *viz.* Achaia. Indeed, I Cor. is addressed to the church which is at Corinth, the capital of Achaia, whereas usually Paul writes to a given community—or to communities limited to one region (Gal. 1:2)—and not to all the churches at the same time. Moreover, it clearly results from the text of the epistle that it is addressed to a given Church that has specific problems.

We then conclude that in Thess. 1:8 also the Apostle means that the news of the Thessalonians' faith has spread not only to Macedonia and Achaia, but also in all the churches founded by him. This is quite possible since Paul used to inquire about the communities he had founded through emissaries from among his companions (I Cor. 4:17; 16:10, 12; II Cor. 8:6, 23; 12:18; Phil. 2:9; I Thess. 3:2, 6). It was thus quite natural that such churches would be informed of any progress in their founder's activity.

At this point we would like to render fully v.8 according to what we consider to be its most adequate meaning: "For, after we had left Thessalonica, we made the word of the Lord (*i.e.*, the gospel) resound in Macedonia (especially Beroea) and Achaia; and we have also told them of your faith in God. Yet the news of your faith has gone beyond these two provinces; it has indeed reached all the churches we founded, by way of emissaries we sent to inquire of their status."

We shall finally deal with the syntactical oddity mentioned above, namely the use of "ἀλλά—but" instead of "ἀλλὰ καί—but also"

---

[37]The opening of I Cor. reads as follows: "Paul, called by the will of God to be an apostle of Christ Jesus, and our brother Sosthenes, to the church of God which is at Corinth, to those sanctified in Christ Jesus, called to be saints, together with all those who *in every place* call on the name of our Lord Jesus Christ, both their Lord and ours: Grace to you and peace from God our Father and the Lord Jesus Christ" (vv.1-3).

in conjunction with "οὐ μόνον—not only." Regarding this, we
must remember that Paul did not write his letters himself, but dictated
them to scribes. That was a very common practice in those days,
since writing on parchment was not an easy task and was performed
by skilled persons called scribes or amanuenses. Let us then visualize
our Apostle dictating the letter to one of his scribes. When he arrived
at the end of v.7, he intended—as we have shown above—to explain
how the faithful of Macedonia and Achaia heard of what had
taken place in Thessalonica. He started by saying that this happened
while the word of the Lord was being preached there. At the mention of the spreading of the gospel Paul was carried away and wanted
to underline that the word of the Lord was preached not only in
Macedonia and Achaia, but also in many other places. But at that
point he remembered that his topic was the spreading of the news
concerning the Thessalonians' faith, and thus he said that, in every
place reached by his gospel, this news was heard. This will explain
the absence of "καί—also" after "ἀλλά—but," since—as we have
just indicated—with "ἐν παντὶ τόπῳ—everywhere" a new phrase
started. Our view is confirmed by the fact that the last part of the
verse, "so that—ὥστε—we need not say anything," logically follows
the immediately preceding: "but your faith in God has gone forth
everywhere," and does not follow the first part of the verse. Indeed
Paul wanted to say that he had no need to make any further comment regarding the Thessalonians' faith, and obviously not regarding
his preaching activity.

The definition of faith as being πρὸς τὸν Θεόν appears only here
in the New Testament. This reflects the influence of the idea of the
movement towards God resulting from the repentance of the heathens and
their return to the living and true God. Now this idea is found in the
following verse: καὶ πῶς ἐπεστρέψατε πρὸς τὸν Θεόν.

The apostle ends v.8 by saying that there was no need for
him to add anything concerning the faith of the Thessalonians,
since what could he have said more than that all the churches
founded by him were aware of their faith and that they
even took them as an example!

v.9. αὐτοὶ γὰρ περὶ ἡμῶν ἀπαγγέλλουσιν ὁποίαν εἴσοδον ἔσχομεν
πρὸς ὑμᾶς, καὶ πῶς ἐπεστρέψατε
πρὸς τὸν Θεὸν ἀπὸ τῶν εἰδώλων
δουλεύειν Θεῷ ζῶντι καὶ ἀληθινῷ,

For they themselves report concerning us what
an entrance/welcome we had among you and
how you turned to God from idols, to serve
the living and true God,

Paul returns here, after the parenthesis of v.8, to the idea
he left in v.7, saying that the example the Thessalonians rep-
resent is clearly shown in the fact that the faithful of Macedonia and Achaia are telling of what has happened in
Thessalonica. Yet in Paul's eyes the event is not limited to
the Thessalonians' faith, since this is simply the positive result (see v.6) of the preaching undertaken by the Apostle
and his companions (see v.5). Thus he makes clear that what
the Macedonian and Achaian Christians are reporting about
embraces the preaching of the gospel as well as the Thessalonians' faith. In fact the first part of the report concerns
the coming of the apostles, *i.e.*, their "entrance—εἴσοδον"
into Thessalonica. The word "entrance—εἴσοδος" in conjunction with the apostolic preaching is used only twice in
the whole of the New Testament, and both here, in the same
context (1:9 and 2:1).

That the word "entrance" means the act of preaching follows
from these two considerations: (a) the qualitative relative pronoun
"what sort of—οἷος—or ὁποῖος" appears only twice in our letter, in
1:15: "You know what kind of—οἷοι—men we proved to be among
you for your sake," and here in 1:9: "For they themselves report

concerning us what kind of—ὁποίαν—entrance/welcome we had among you"; hence the parallelism of thought; (b) in 2:1-2 we read: "For you yourselves know, brethren, that our entrance/visit—εἴσοδον—to you was not in vain; but though we had already suffered and been shamefully treated at Philippi, as you know, we *had courage* in our God *to declare to you the gospel of God* in the face of great opposition." It is quite clear that Paul himself explains "entrance—εἴσοδος" with his declaring the gospel of God to the Thessalonians.

However, the reported news includes also the result of the apostles' preaching, namely "how you turned to God from idols, to serve the living and true God." The verb ἐπιστρέφω which means "to return, to come back" is usually used in the Septuagint to render the Hebrew verb *shûb*. This verb has the meaning of changing one's course from one direction to another, and that on the physical as well as mental level; hence, the idea of repentance or return to God from a way of life without (far from) Him, which *shûb* endorsed. All this explains the frequent use of ἐπιστρέφω in the Book of Acts to speak of the heathens' acceptance of the Christian faith. "And the residents of Lydda and Sharon saw him, and they turned to the Lord—ἐπέστρεψαν ἐπὶ τὸν κύριον" (Acts 9:35; see also 15:19; 26:20). In some instances we read that the return to God is from—ἀπό—the previous situation (14:15 and 26:18).

Our text tells us that the Thessalonians returned/turned "to God from the idols—πρὸς[38] τὸν Θεὸν ἀπὸ τῶν εἰδώλων" (see Acts 14:15). This is a clear indication that the majority of the faithful in Thessalonica were originally heathens,[39] since the Apostle would not have addressed Jews in this way. Whence it results that the first thing asked from non-Jews upon their acceptance of the gospel was to cease

---

[38]Both prepositions πρός and ἐπί governing an accusative give the meaning of direction.

[39]See the Introduction and Acts 15:3 where we find the expression "the conversion of the Gentiles—ἐπιστροφὴν τῶν ἐθνῶν."

worshipping the other gods which are mere idols. With this, the first aim or result[40] of their leaving the idols becomes to serve the living and true God—δουλεύειν Θεῷ ζῶντι καὶ ἀληθινῷ.

Although the Greek text literally reads: "a living and true God," we preferred to use the definite article in our translation for the following considerations:

1) Those who translate our passage without the definite article advocate that Paul has just used the definite article—τὸν Θεόν—in v.8, and that if he intended to use it here he would have done so. Our objection to this point is based on that after each use of the verb ἐπιστρέφω in the sense of returning to God, we always find the expression ἐπὶ τὸν Θεόν (Acts 15:19; 26:18, 20), or ἐπὶ τὸν κύριον (Acts 9:35; 11:21). Interesting here is that the only exception to this rule is precisely "ἐπὶ Θεὸν ζῶντα" of Acts 14:15 (see further below our third point). Our conclusion is that ἐπιστρέφω ἐπὶ τὸν Θεόν was a *terminus technicus* for the acceptance of the Christian faith by the heathens (see Acts 14:15; 26:18).

2) Again, those advocating the translation without the definite article say that such translation renders Paul's intention to emphasize the point that this new God for the heathens is a living and true one in comparison with the idols that are dead and vain. However, we think that the definite article does not negate this idea, but rather stresses it by saying that this God is alone the living and true One.

3) Finally, a study of the use of Θεὸς ζῶν in the New Testament will show it always used without the definite article[41] except in the first gospel (Mt. 16:16 and 26:63).[42] Thus we conclude that the use of this expression in the early church reflected its use in the Septuagint. Anyway, it is enough that it appears in this form in the Pauline letters in order for us to affirm that this was the Apostle's use of it.

Δουλεύειν is the translation of the Hebrew verb '*abad* which carries both meanings: to serve and to worship, since God's service is especially shown forth in His worship. Now the God whom the heathens started worshipping as a result of Paul's preaching is none but the living and true God. And since the expression "the living God—Θεῷ ζῶντι" is common in the New Testament,[43] the stress seems to be here on

---

[40]The infinitive after an indicative in Greek indicates aim or result.

[41]Acts 14:15; Rom. 9:26; II Cor. 3:3; 6:16; I Tim. 3:15; 4:10; Heb. 3:12; 9:14; 10:31; 12:22; I Pet. 1:23.

[42]The Book of Revelation has "Θεοῦ ζῶντος" in 7:2 and "τοῦ Θεοῦ τοῦ ζῶντος" in 15:7.

[43]The intention of this expression is to say that God is living when

the attribute "true—ἀληθινῷ," especially that the latter does not appear except here in all of Paul's writings. The Apostle's intention is then that God whom the Thessalonians now serve is not only the living God, but that this living God is indeed true compared to the idols which are nothing (I Cor. 10:19), even non-existing (I Cor. 8:4) in Paul's eyes.

However, all that we have said about the first aim or result of the heathens' return from the idols to God, *viz.* the worship and service of the living and true God, is not enough to make of them Christians, since the Jews render this worship and yet are not Christians; hence the importance of v.10, which is linked to our verse with the conjunction "and—καί."

v.10. καὶ ἀναμένειν τόν υἱόν αὐτοῦ ἐκ τῶν οὐρανῶν, ὃν ἤγειρεν ἐκ τῶν νεκρῶν, Ἰησοῦν τόν ῥυόμενον ἡ- μᾶς ἐκ τῆς ὀργῆς τῆς ἐρχομένης.

and to wait for His Son from heaven, whom He raised from the dead, Jesus who delivers us from the wrath to come.

The main word in this verse is "Jesus," especially since it is used without either of its two essential qualifying terms: Christ or the Lord. In both epistles to the Thessalonians the term "Jesus" does not appear by itself except here and in I Thess. 4:14, where also—as we shall see—the topic is a compendium of Christian faith. And this Jesus is first of all

---

compared with other deities which are nothing but empty idols begotten by human imagination.

the Son of the living and true God. It is extremely important
that we find already here—in the first Christian text that
has reached us, which was written around 50 A.D.—that one
of the main features of Paul's preaching was Jesus' sonship
to God (see our comments on 1:1 above). Of even greater
importance is the fact that the Apostle does not comment
on this point, nor does he justify it; as we have seen earlier
(1:3), this is a proof that the point in question is at the
heart of the Christian message and thus does not need further
elaboration.

However, our relationship to Jesus is not limited to our
belief that he is the Son of God; it embraces especially our
waiting for him from heaven. Thus we see that our expectation of Jesus' coming is the first aspect that differentiates the
believer in that his whole life reaches out for that moment.
This is the way in which the believer confirms that Jesus
the Son of God is actually the fullness and meaning of his
life. And the Lord Jesus will come "from heaven—ἐκ τῶν
οὐρανῶν." In the New Testament "heaven" indicated God's
abode, *i.e.*, the place filled with His glory. To say then that
Jesus will come from heaven (see 4:16) is to say that he is
now abiding in divine glory.

Jesus' coming has to do with "the wrath to come." This
expression is taken from the Old Testament prophets who
used it to tell their people that God's coming will not neces-
sarily mean the overpowering of the nations and the glorification of the Israelite people, but that it will be "a day of
wrath" (Zeph. 1:18) in case the people, and especially their
leaders, are carrying on their evil deeds. The emphasis on
the idea of "wrath" derives from the fact that God is holy
and that His holiness cannot bear sin but consumes it totally.
Thus the day of the coming of God started to carry with it the
idea of the wrath to come, in that judgment is in His hand
and He will judge all beings. Due to his sin (see Rom. 3:9-12)
man always sees God's judgment under the image of a coming
wrath. Therefore the expression "the wrath to come" means

God's just judgment at the end of days. And since we said
that Jesus' coming was in close relation to the last judgment
(see also I Thess. 3:13), the believer has a continuous hope
that the Lord Jesus will save him from the divine wrath, in
that "God made Christ Jesus our wisdom, our *righteousness*
and *sanctification* and redemption" (I Cor. 1:30).

But our faith and our hope are linked to a specific past
event[44] constituting the roots of our being Christians, *viz.*,
that God raised His Son Jesus from the dead. Our epistle
confirms that there were in the early church two ways of
speaking of the resurrection of the Lord Jesus: the first, that
God raised Him, and the second, that He died and rose again
as in 4:14. Whereas the latter form underlines the event of
the resurrection and that it is linked to the historical death
of the person of Jesus, the former emphasizes that the resurrection of Jesus Christ is a divine event/action, not a magical
trick. And God's raising of Jesus from the dead is the proof
that He is the master of the living and the dead, and that
He, not death and its power, has the last word.

All of the above clearly shows that the compendium of
the gospel lies for Paul in the resurrection of Jesus, which is
a past event (see "raised—ἤγειρεν"), as well as in His
coming from heaven on the judgment day to deliver us from
the divine wrath, which is a future event (see "and to wait
for—καὶ ἀναμένειν"). Thus the being of the believer, which
lies in the gospel, has two essential points of reference: the
resurrection of Jesus and His coming. And neither is of this
world. Therefore, the faithful is not of this world. Yet he is
in it, reminding everybody that "true" life is first and last in
Jesus, since it originates in His resurrection and reaches out to
where he is, *viz.*, in His Father's bosom.

---

[44] Note that the verb "raised—ἤγειρεν" is in the aorist.

CHAPTER TWO

v.1. Αὐτοὶ γὰρ οἴδατε, ἀδελφοί, τὴν εἴσοδον ἡμῶν πρὸς ὑμᾶς, ὅτι οὐ κενὴ
γέγονεν.

For you yourselves know, brethren, that our
entrance/coming/visit to you was not in vain.

In chapter two the Apostle comes back to the subject of
his evangelizing of the Thessalonians, which he left at the
end of 1:5 for a digression on their acceptance of the gospel
(1:6-10).[1] But this time Paul will deal in detail with how
he brought the gospel to them, in the first twelve verses
of our chapter. This detailed account shows how the Jews
in Thesalonica tried to undermine Paul's work by using
slander against his person as well as his apostleship. They
were to continue to use this method wherever the Apostle
endeavored to bring the gospel, as can be clearly seen from
his later epistles—I Cor., II Cor., Gal., Phil. The same situation is reflected in the Book of Acts. This explains why
Paul felt it necessary to devote quite a long passage in each
of the above mentioned epistles to defending himself as
well as his apostolicity, by reminding the faithful of all that

---

[1]The link between 1:5 and 2:1 is obvious also on stylistic grounds.
The verb "you know—οἴδατε" found in 1:5 does not appear again until
chapter two, where it is encountered no less than four times in the first
twelve verses.

happened among them when he came to them and of how
he behaved in their midst. Sometimes he even found it necessary to base his apologia on pertinent personal data (Gal.
1-2 and especially II Cor. 10-12). That is why Paul leaves
the subject of how the Thessalonians accepted the faith—
which is the second part of what the faithful in Macedonia
and Achaia are talking about (v.9b)—to resume, this time
in detail, the account of his preaching activity in Thessalonica.

Paul starts the apologia for his apostolicity by reminding
the Thessalonian brethren that his "coming/entrance" to
them, *i.e.*, his evangelizing them, was not "in vain—κενή."
This Greek adjective means properly: empty, and figur-
atively: without meaning, vain, without result, fruitless.
Thus the Apostle reminds the Thessalonians ("For you
yourselves know . . .") that his activity among them was not
fruitless. The proof was, as we have seen, that quite a number accepted the true faith (1:9-10). Our conviction that
the faith of the Thessalonians is the fruit that crowned the
Apostle's efforts stems also from the fact that the word κενόν
appears only one other time in our epistle, in the following
context: "For this reason, when I could bear it no longer,
I sent that I might know your faith—τὴν πίστιν ὑμῶν—
for fear that somehow the tempter had tempted you and that
our labor would be in vain—εἰς κενόν" (3:5).

The use of the perfect γέγονεν here (the first two chapters are full
of the same verb, but in the aorist—ἐγενήθη, ἐγενήθημεν, ἐγενήθητε)
indicates Paul's intention to emphasize that his preaching was not in vain
and that its outcome. *i.e.*, the Thessalonians' faith, was still felt at the
time of his writing this epistle (see 3:6).

v.2. ἀλλὰ προπαθόντες καὶ ὑβρισθέν-
τες καθὼς οἴδατε ἐν Φιλίπποις ἐ-
παρρησιασάμεθα ἐν τῷ Θεῷ ἡμῶν

λαλῆσαι πρὸς ὑμᾶς τὸ εὐαγγέλιον τοῦ Θεοῦ ἐν πολλῷ ἀγῶνι.

but though we had already suffered and been
shamefully treated at Philippi, as you know,
we had courage in our God to declare to you
the gospel of God in the face of great opposition.

The conjunction "ἀλλά—but, however" either negates a
previous positive statement or confirms a negative one. Thus,
the logically expected here was either a confirmation that
the gospel preaching had been fruitful, or rather the enumeration of some points proving this, since Paul had referred to the Thessalonians' memory in the previous verse
(οἴδατε—you know). Instead, the Apostle stuns us with a
sudden shift to the mention of events that had taken place
before his arrival in Thessalonica. He intended, as it were,
to prove the effectiveness of his preaching in that city not
on the basis of the fruits, but on that of the "seeds" of this
preaching, if we may so say. Thus he says that he had
previously suffered (προπαθόντες) and been shamefully
treated at Philippi. That this was the Apostle's intention is
shown (in the original Greek text) in his including "καθὼς
οἴδατε—as you know" immediately after the verbs of suffering and maltreatment, and before naming the place where
these happened: "ἐν Φιλίπποις—at Philippi."

In Paul's eyes then, his boldness to proclaim the gospel of
God in Thessalonica *in the face of great opposition*, and in
spite of the *suffering* and *insults* he had met in Philippi, is
enough proof for the truthfulness of his apostolicity.

We do know from the Book of Acts that Paul suffered
beating and imprisonment in the city of Philippi (16:22-24).
Now this kind of treatment was shameful and insulting when

inflicted on a Roman citizen, which Paul was, as appears from Acts 16:35-39. It is indeed known that a citizen of Rome and its surroundings had in the Roman Empire certain privileges that included exemption from undergoing physical maltreatment and torture (see Acts 22:25). In case he was condemned to the capital punishment, then beheading was the rule, which saved him from being tortured to death. It is also known that, when Roman authority spread into many provinces which became fully part of the Roman Empire, emperors used to gratify some of the main cities by bestowing upon their inhabitants "Roman citizenship." Among such cities seems to have been Tarsus, where the Apostle Paul was born (see Acts 21:39 and 22:27-28).

Thus, in spite of the suffering and insult, Paul had the courage "in God—ἐν τῷ Θεῷ" to resume his way and proclaim the gospel to the Thessalonians "ἐν πολλῷ ἀγῶνι— in the face of great opposition." In the first century A.D. the word ἀγών meant every sports competition taking place in a theater or arena. Paul who grew up in Tarsus, a very important city in the province of Cilicia (in the mid-southern part of present-day Turkey), was naturally influenced by city life. This explains the frequent use of sports imagery in his writings: the athlete's behavior (I Cor. 9:25), running (I Cor. 9:24, 26; Phil. 3:13-14), boxing (I Cor. 9:26), athletic effort in general (Phil. 1:27 and 4:3, where we find the verb συναθλέω), the victor's wreath (I Cor. 9:25; Phil. 4:1; I Thess. 2:19). Therefore, every time the Apostle spoke of any kind of effort for the gospel's sake—even when he meant a spiritual one (Rom. 5:30; Col. 4:12)—the imagery of athletic competition flooded his mind. Thus the use of "ἐν πολλῷ ἀγῶνι—with much effort/in the face of great opposition" is an indication of the extreme exertion he underwent in Thessalonica after his bitter experience in Philippi, especially in that this was at the hands of the Jews, "his brethren, his kinsmen by race" as he calls them in Rom. 9:3. We conclude that the Apostle meant by "ἐν πολλῷ ἀγῶνι" that his continuous endeavor for the sake of the gospel (see Phil. 3:13) took an extremely painful aspect in the city of Thessalonica.

vv. 3-4. ἡ γὰρ παράκλησις ἡμῶν οὐκ ἐκ πλάνης οὐδὲ ἐξ ἀκαθαρσίας οὐδὲ ἐν δόλῳ, ἀλλὰ καθὼς δεδοκιμάσμεθα ὑπὸ τοῦ Θεοῦ πιστευθῆναι τὸ εὐαγγέλιον οὕτως λαλοῦμεν, οὐ ὡς ἀνθρώποις ἀρέσκοντες, ἀλλὰ Θεῷ τῷ δοκιμάζοντι τὰς καρδίας ἡμῶν.

For our appeal does not spring from error or uncleanness, nor it is made with guile; but just as we have been approved by God to be entrusted with the gospel, so we speak, not to please men, but to please God who tests our hearts.

In these two verses Paul explains the reason for his courage/boldness to resume his preaching in spite of difficulties. And the reason—which we have already guessed when we read in v.2 that the Apostle had courage "in God"— is that God had tested him and found him worthy to be entrusted with the gospel. Therefore his preaching does not spring from error or uncleanness, nor is it with guile.

Before starting our detailed commentary on these verses we would like to draw attention to two important facts. The first is that Paul was not satisfied with giving the positive answer of v.4, but he made a point of making first a very forceful negative statement: "... neither from error, nor from uncleanness, nor in guile." This indicates that his opponents in Thessalonica have spread among the faithful there disparaging accusations that belittled him and that this news reached his ears.

The second point is that the only verb in both verses "λαλοῦμεν— we speak" (v.4) is in he present indicative, while the absence of εἶναι (to be) in v.3 indicates that there also the idea is one of present indicative. Thus, in his apologia, Paul generalized his statement by saying that this was the style he always followed. Our opinion is further confirmed by the use of the temporal adverb "ever—ποτε" in v.5 and the expression "nor from others—οὔτε ἀπ᾽ ἄλλων" in v.6 (see our comments at that point).

The conclusion is that the Apostle's words here embrace his whole missionary activity. Thus, such accusations (v.3) against him started right at the beginning of his missionary work and not merely in Thessalonica, which gives us a good idea of the difficulties Paul's opponents created for him to hinder his work in God's service.[2]

But what would be the meaning of these accusations against our Apostle? Πλάνη means error/erring/going astray. Thus, when saying that his appeal is not out of error— ἐκ πλάνης—Paul means that his preaching does not have an incorrect/erring starting point. But still, what is precisely meant by πλάνη as used by the Apostle Paul? A detailed study of his use of this word shows that it means: false teaching, deceiving teaching, a teaching stemming not from God but from being away from Him; in other words, the understanding and belief which were common among the Gentiles.

In Rom. 1:27 we find the straight-forward statement that the heathens' ungodly way of life (1:26-32) is the due penalty for their error—τῆς πλάνης αὐτῶν. It clearly appears from the context that "error" means the being away from God and the worship of man-created idols (1:21-23, 25).

---

[2]Regarding these opponents see the Introduction.

In I Cor. 6:9-11 we read the following: "... Do you not know that the unrighteous will not inherit the kingdom of God? *Do not be deceived/in error*—μὴ πλανᾶσθε. Neither the immoral, *nor idolators*, nor adulterers, nor homosexuals, nor thieves, nor the greedy, nor drunkards, nor revilers, nor robbers will inherit the kingdom of God. *And such were some of you.* But you were washed, you were sanctified, you were justified in the name of the Lord Jesus Christ and in the Spirit of our God." Here also the concept of "error" is in intimate relation to idolatry, since: (a) the intent of v.11: "And such were some of you. But you were washed ..." is that through baptism the Corinthians were taken away from their previous life into one of holiness and righteousness; now it is well known that their vast majority were heathens;[3] (b) the series of nouns in vv.9-10 is a striking parallel to those found in Rom. 1:29-31; (c) one of these nouns is εἰδωλολάτραι, *i.e.*, idolaters.

I Cor. 15:33-34 reads: "*Do not be deceived/in error*—μὴ πλανᾶσθε. Bad companions ruin good morals. Come to your right mind, and sin no more. For some have no knowledge of God—ἀγνωσίαν Θεοῦ. I say this to your shame." Here also Paul links error to the non-knowledge of God, *i.e.*, heathenism.

In II Cor. 6:8 the Apostle argues that he is truthful and correct in his preaching, against the charge of his being a deceiver: ὡς πλάνοι καὶ ἀληθεῖς. We do know from him (Rom. 1:18, 25) that the heathens suppress the truth—τὴν ἀλήθειαν—by their wickedness, and that they exchanged the truth about/of God—τὴν ἀλήθειαν τοῦ Θεοῦ—for a lie—ἐν τῷ ψεύδει. Compare also with Eph. 4:14-15 where the opposition is made between error—πλάνη—and speaking the truth—ἀληθεύοντες. Compare as well with II Thess. 2:11-12 where Paul compares the effect of deceit/error—ἐνέργειαν πλάνης—and the belief of what is false—πιστεῦσαι τῷ ψεύδει—on the one hand, with the non-believing of the truth—οἱ μὴ πιστεύσαντες τῇ ἀληθείᾳ—on the other.

Gal. 6:7 reads: "Do not be deceived—μὴ πλανᾶσθε. God is not (may not be) mocked." It is obvious that such a warning is directed to people of heathen origin, *i.e.*, having had no previous knowledge of the living God.

From I Tim. 4:1 and 6:10 it clearly appears that the idea of "error" is fully related to apostasy, while in II Tim. 3:12-14 we find that both deceivers and deceived are the evil men (v.13) who

---

[3]See virtually any commentary on I Cor.

do not live a godly life in Christ Jesus (v.12) and who do not continue in the correct teachings they have learned (v.14).

Finally Tit. 3:3-5 indicates that error/deceit is related to the heathen period in man's life, *i.e.*, before the Lord's epiphany and knowledge of him.

The second accusation against the Apostle is uncleanness or impurity—ἀκαθαρσία. A similar detailed study of this word in the Pauline writings will show that the meaning is the heathen way of life.

At the end of his dealing with the error of the heathens (Rom. 1:1-23) Paul says: "Therefore God gave them up in the lusts of their hearts to impurity—εἰς ἀκαθαρσίαν—to the dishonoring of their bodies among themselves" (v.24). See also Eph. 4:17-19.

In many texts ἀκαθαρσία appears in opposition to holiness—ἁγιασμός—which is a quality of those who believed in the living God.[4] See Rom. 6:19; I Cor. 7:14; I Thess. 4:5-7.

In his endeavor to convince the Corinthians that there is no partnership between *believer and unbeliever*, between righteousness and iniquity, beween *the temple of God and idols*—since they themselves are the temple of God—(II Cor. 6:14-16), Paul quotes God's words in Isaiah: ". . . Therefore come out from them, and be separate from them, says the Lord, and touch nothing *unclean*—ἀκαθάρτου; then I will welcome you" (v.17; see Is. 52:11).

In II Cor. 12:21 ἀκαθαρσία is at the head of a long list of things the believer is asked to repent of. Compare with Gal. 5:19.

In Gal. 5:19 ἀκαθαρσία is quoted along with idolatry—εἰδω-λολατρία (v.20) among the works of the flesh—σάρξ. Now "the works of the flesh" are in full opposition to the works of the Spirit (Gal. 5:22ff.). And it is only clear from the epistle to the Galatians that the Spirit—πνεῦμα—represents the new life in Christ, while σάρξ is linked to the heathen way of life among the Galatians before their faith in Jesus (3:2-5; 5:16-17).

---

[4]The notion of holiness in the Old Testament is a central one. It is used to differentiate between Israel and the nations: "For I am the Lord your God; consecrate yourselves therefore, and be holy, for I am holy . . . For I am the Lord who brought you up out of the land of Egypt, to be your God; you shall therefore be holy, for I am holy" (Lev. 11:44-45); "And the Lord said to Moses: Say to all the congregation of Israel, You shall be holy; for I the Lord your God am holy . . . Do not turn to idols or make for yourselves molten gods: I am the Lord your God" (Lev. 19:1-4).

Finally Col. 3:5 clearly indicates that uncleanness or impurity—
ἀκαθαρσία—is one of the aspects of idolatry—εἰδωλολατρία.
See also Eph. 5:3-5.

Therefore πλάνη and ἀκαθαρσία are in intimate relation to each other, and both refer to idolatry. Whereas
πλάνη carries the meaning of false heathen teachings, ἀκαθαρσία indicates the heathen way of life that is unclean
due to its being away from the true God. That which πλάνη
reflects on the mental level of doctrines, ἀκαθαρσία expresses on the ethical level of daily life. Thus, in the Apostle's
eyes, the heathen is an erring being in the full sense of the
word.

However, the more important conclusion is that the source
of slander and accusations against Paul are definitely the
Jews, since only they would be interested in discrediting him
before the Thessalonians by presenting him as at odds
with the other apostles and the leaders of the mother church
of Jerusalem. Thus, their intention is to show him scornful
of Old Testament law and championing heathen teachings.
It appears clearly from the rest of Paul's epistles that the
Jews will continue to follow the same tactics: raise doubts
regarding the truthfulness of his apostolicity and the correctness of his teaching.

As to the third accusation against the Apostle, it is guile/
duplicity—δόλος (see also II Cor. 4:2 and especially 12:16).
This accusation is the meanest since its intent is to put Paul
in the garb of a false apostle—ψευδαπόστολος. Indeed,
at one point the idea of guile/duplicity appears to qualify
false apostles—ψευδαπόστολοι—as being deceitful workers—ἐργάται δόλιοι—who disguise themselves as apostles
of Christ—μετασχηματιζόμενοι εἰς ἀποστόλους Χριστοῦ (II Cor. 11:13), while another time it appears in relation to the preaching of God's word (II Cor. 4:2). Such
an accusation thus to a certain extent epitomizes the first
two, in that it challenges Paul's claim to be an apostle.

Similar accusations continued to harass him all his life. That explains his constant concern to defend the truthfulness of his apostolicity, as is shown in I Corinthians, II Corinthians, Galatians and Philippians.

Le us look more specifically into the prepositions used in v.3: "For our appeal is not from error—ἐκ πλάνης—nor from uncleanness—ἐξ ἀκαθαρσίας, nor in guile—ἐν δόλῳ." The preposition ἐκ[5] indicates the source or origin; Paul used it with the two words which indicate, as shown above, the heathen doctrine and way of life, *i.e.*, the supposed heathen origin/source of the Apostle's teachings. As for the preposition ἐν before δόλῳ, it indicates that the preaching was not in guile, and thus ἐν δόλῳ refers to Paul's behavior or the *way* he used to spread his teaching.

After refuting the accusations against him, the Apostle confirms their lack of foundation by referring to the fact that God had already examined him thoroughly and found him worthy to be entrusted with the gospel. He continues to speak—*i.e.*, preach as we have seen in 2:2—on the basis of this approval, heeding not men's approval but to please God who alone tests the hearts. "Καρδία—heart" does not mean here the biological organ that pumps blood into the arteries. It is rather the Septuagint rendering of the Hebrew noun *leb* which, in the Old Testament, represents the center of the deep inner being: whence spring all of man's thoughts and behavior and in which his encounter with the Lord takes place.

v.5. οὔτε γάρ ποτε ἐν λόγῳ κολακείας ἐγενήθημεν, καθὼς οἴδατε, οὔτε ἐν προφάσει πλεονεξίας, Θεὸς μάρτυς,

For we never used (did not ever use) either

---

[5]Written ἐξ before a vowel.

words of flattery, as you know, or a cloak
for greed, as God is witness;

The Apostle continues his thought by trying to prove
what he just said, namely that he is trying to please God,
not men. He thus reminds the Thessalonians of something
they know only too well (here again Paul uses "καθὼς
οἴδατε—as you know"): he did not come to them "ἐν λόγῳ
κολακείας—with words of flattery." The term "κολα-
κεία—flattery," found only here in the New Testament,
means the sweet words used to impress the hearer with the
intention of getting a profit out of him as well as his
benevolence, without being interested in conveying to him
the truth. This is definitely what the Apostle intended to
say, since this idea follows immediately his denial of being
interested in pleasing men (v.4).

Though he appeals to the Thessalonians' memory ("as
you know"), Paul introduces before the verb "ἐγενήθημεν—were/behaved/arrived" the particle "ποτε—ever."
This indicates that, at that precise moment, the Apostle was
so disturbed by the repeated accusations against him that he
had to make it clear: nothing whatsoever of what he is
accused of has ever taken place, either at Thessalonica or
elsewhere (see v.6: "nor did we seek glory from men,
whether from you or *from others* ..."). This in turn confirms our earlier conclusion that Paul's statement in v.3 is
general and applies to all the stages of his missionary activity.

The Apostle proceeds saying: "... or a cloak for greed,
as God is witness." The word πρόφασις means an ill motive,
while πλεονεξία signifies greed. Now, if Paul appealed to
the Thessalonians' recollection ("as you know") regarding
the words of flattery, these being an external act that falls
under the range of human discernment, a greedy motive is
purely mental and can be known only to God. Therefore

the Apostle uses God Himself as his witness in this regard:
"God is witness to the truth of what I am saying."

Before proceeding to the following verse, we would like here to draw
attention to an important point. The concept of greed under both forms,
nominal (πλεονεξία) as well as adjectival (πλεονεκτής), usually appears in the Pauline writings as a heathen practice (Rom. 1:29; I Cor.
5:10-11; 6:10; Eph. 4:19; 5:3, 5; Col. 3:5). Now, we have seen earlier
in studying v.3 that the word "guile—δόλος" had a direct link to the idea
of false/incorrect teaching. Thus the expression "ἐν προφάσει πλεονεξίας—
a cloak for greed" in v.5 is parallel to the statement "οὐκ ἐκ πλάνης οὐδὲ
ἐξ ἀκαθαρσίας" of v.3, while "ἐν λόγῳ κολακείας—words of flattery"
is parallel to "οὐδὲ ἐν δόλῳ—nor with guile." It then appears that, after
proving the correctness of his preaching on the basis of God's calling him
and entrusting him with the gospel, Paul reaffirms this with a proof taken
from his behavior during his missionary activity.

v.6. οὔτε ζητοῦντες ἐξ ἀνθρώπων δόξαν, οὔτε ἀφ᾽ ὑμῶν οὔτε ἀπ᾽ ἄλλων,

nor do we seek glory from men, whether from
you or from others,

It is obvious that the idea of this verse is parallel to that which we
read at the end of v.4: "... not to please men, but to please God ...," namely
it is a proof from the Apostle's behavior that his previous statement is true.
This is a confirmation of the parallelism in meaning between vv.3 and 5
which we have just indicated. Thus vv.5 and 6 appear to be a reaffirma-
tion of vv.3 and 4.

The use of the participle "οὔτε ζητοῦντες—nor are we
seeking" in the present (continuous) tense emphasizes that,
here also, the Apostle Paul's vision at that moment does not
stop at Thessalonica but goes beyond to the whole of his
prior activity. The Apostle is giving us, as it were, an image
of his usual behavior during his activity for the sake of
spreading God's word. Anyway, this is also confirmed by

the use of "or from others" with "whether from you" after
he says: "nor are we seeking glory from men."

The word "δόξαν—glory" means here either approval
or applause—if we take it with the idea of pleasing men
of v.4—or honor or glorification—if we understand it along
with "ἐν βάρει εἶναι—to make our weight felt" of the
following verse. But since the relation between approval and
glorification is quite close, we will not lose much time on
this issue. We will limit ourselves to expressing our inclina-
tion toward the second alternative, and that because:
(a) δόξα usually bears the meaning of greatness and
glorification, and (b) verse 6 is linked not only in meaning
(as is the case with v.4)[6] but also grammatically to the first
part of v.7.

The preposition "ἐκ or ἐξ—out of" usually points to the
source or first origin of something, whereas "ἀπό—from"
indicates the immediate origin. Thus Paul's intention is to
say: I do not seek glory out of—ἐξ—men, i.e., a glory whose
ultimate source is human, a glory of the human kind, a
human glory . . . and that, neither from you—ἀφ᾽ ὑμῶν—
nor from others—ἀπ᾽ ἄλλων, i.e., whoever might be the
one bestowing it on me, you or anyone else.

v.7a-b. δυνάμενοι ἐν βάρει εἶναι ὡς Χριστοῦ ἀπόστολοι· ἀλλὰ ἐγενήθημεν
ἤπιοι ἐν μέσῳ ἡμῶν.

though we might have made felt our im-

---

[6]Regarding the parallelism between the verses 6 and 4, see Gal. 1:10b:
". . . Or am I trying/seeking—ζητῶ (see I Thess. 1:6) to please men—
ἀνθρώποις ἀρέσκειν (see I Thess. 1:4)?"

portance (weight) as apostles of Christ, but
we behaved gently (were gentle) among you.

The manuscripts that include our epistle are not in full agreement regarding the reading of the word ἥπιοι. In some—which are the more important—
we find νήπιοι, while in others we read ἥπιοι. A textual critique based on
the possibility of an error in copying does not allow a clear-cut choice, since
ἥπιοι may have originated from νήπιοι through haplography,[7] while the
opposite may be accounted for by dittography.[8] We shall therefore undertake here a detailed study that will, we believe, justify our preference for
"ἥπιοι—gentle" over "νήπιοι—babes." Our starting point will be our position that the passage vv.7c-8 ("like a nurse . . . you had become very dear to
us—ὡς ἐὰν τροφός . . . ἀγαπητοὶ ἡμῖν ἐγενήθητε") is a grammatical
unit, more specifically one sentence. These are the reasons:

1) In the Pauline writings the particle "οὕτως—so also, thus" is found
without exception either in a parallel use with the expression "as" under
its different forms: ὡς, ὥσπερ, καθάπερ, καθώς; or in a clear conjunction with the preceding (Rom. 6:11; I Cor. 2:11; 14:9; 15:42; I Thess.
4:14).[9] Thus οὕτως is always for Paul either comparative (so also) or
final (thus, therefore), and has never the meaning "to that extent."[10]
Consequently we believe that there is no reason here for an exception and
that οὕτως in v.8 means "so also" in comparison with "ὡς—as" of the
previous verse. Thus οὕτως is to be taken with the indicative εὐδοκοῦμεν
and not with the participle ὁμειρόμενοι.[11]

2) The noun "τροφός—nurse" and the verb "ὁμείρομαι—to show
affection, to care lovingly" (as present participle in our text) appear each
only once, namely here, in the whole New Testament. As for the verb
"θάλπω—to embrace, to care" it is found only here and in Eph. 5:29, an
epistle written at least fourteen years later than I Thessalonians. Therefore
we strongly believe that the words τροφός, θάλπῃ and ὁμειρόμενοι are
in an intimate conjunction with one another: (a) Paul in effect uses them
only here; (b) both verbs fit perfectly with the noun τροφός. In any case,
even those who argue that v.7c is linked to the preceding, i.e., v.7b, admit
that the participle ὁμειρόμενοι of v.8 is related in meaning to v.7c.

3) In the whole passage 2:5-12 the Apostle is talking about past events
and thus uses his verbs in the aorist: ἐγενήθημεν (vv.5, 7, 10), ἐγενήθητε
(v.8) and ἐκηρύξαμεν (v.9). Only θάλπω and εὐδοκέω—and both
appear in the text we are discussing—are in the present. Θάλπῃ, being

---

[7]If the original was: ἐγενήθημεν νήπιοι.

[8]If the original was: ἐγενήθημεν ἥπιοι.

[9]The absence of καί after οὕτως in our text (in contrast to the usual
Pauline usage) can be explained by the inclusion of the conditional ἐὰν
after ὡς as well as by the fact that οὕτως is not immediately followed by
the subject.

[10]At any rate, in classical Greek, when οὕτως has the meaning of "to
that extent" it is usually followed by ὥστε.

[11]Anyhow, οὕτως is always connected to a verb in the Pauline writings.

in the subjunctive mood, does not prove by itself that the idea in v.7c is a general statement. However, if v.7c is to be considered grammatically related to the preceding, *i.e.*, to v.7b which starts with "ἀλλά—but" and includes an aorist, then those who take this stand will have to justify the present tense of εὐδοκοῦμεν. This is quite an impossible task, since to consider v.8 a complete sentence in itself would mean to read it as parallel to v.7b-c and make of it an application of the latter; in this case the Apostle would be saying that, *while he was in Thessalonica,* he *was* well pleased to offer not only the gospel, but also himself, for the sake of the faithful there. Hence, most of the exegetes translate v.8 as if they were reading the imperfect ηὐδοκοῦμεν instead of the present εὐδοκοῦμεν. In fact ηὐδοκοῦμεν is found in some manuscripts[12] due to an effort on the part of some copyists to solve this difficulty.

4) V.9, which starts with "γάρ—for, since" is to be understood as confirming, and thus related to, v.7a for two reasons. The first is linguistic: the similarity between the verb ἐπιβαρέω (v.9) and the expression ἐν βάρει εἶναι (v.7).[13] The second is logical: the Apostle's living out of the work of his hands is not a proof of his gentleness (v.7b), nor of his embracing the Thessalonians (v.7c), nor of his affection for them (v.8), nor of the fact that they have become dear to him (v.8), but rather is meant as a proof that he did not burden the faithful. As for the proof of his gentle behavior (v.7b), he will deal with it in vv.10-12, especially in the passage: "For your know how, like a father with his children, we exhorted each one of you and encouraged you and charged you..." (v.11). Therefore we believe that the verses 7c-8 are a parenthesis where the main idea appears at the end of v.8: the Thessalonians have become dear to Paul (see below).

The passage 7c-8 is thus a sentence in its own right, which means that v.7b is linked to the preceding. And since it starts with "ἀλλά—but," it is only normal that it be in opposition with what preceded it. In that case it is logical to assume that Paul uses the adjective "ἤπιοι—gentle" since it carries an idea in full opposition with the notion of "weight—ἐν βάρει" mentioned immediately before in v.7a.

The presence of "νήπιοι—babes" in a number of manuscripts can be explained through the repetition of the letter "ν" appearing at the end of the immediately preceding ἐγενήθημεν, especially since νήπιος is common in the Pauline writings, whereas ἤπιος is found only one other time[14] in the entire New Testament.

In the first part of v.7 (which is logically linked to what precedes) Paul stresses that, due to his being an apostle of Christ—ὡς Χριστοῦ ἀπόστολοι—in the service of the gospel, he has all the right to exercise some weight—ἐν

---

[12]The aorist εὐδοκήσαμεν is found in the two minuscule manuscripts 33 and 81.

[13]See our comments on this verse below.

[14]II Tim. 2:24.

βάρει εἶναι—during his stay in Thessalonica. The clue to the understanding of the verse is bound to the meaning we give to the expression "ἐν βάρει εἶναι." Since it appears only here in the whole New Testament we have no other choice but to get some insight from the study of the context himself.

A little further and in the same frame of thought (*viz.*, Paul's behavior in Thessalonica) we read: "For you remember our labor and toil, brethren; we worked night and day, that we might not burden any of you—πρὸς τὸ μὴ ἐπιβαρῆσαί τινα ὑμῶν" (v.9). It appears that what is intended by the verb "ἐπιβαρέω—to burden" is the burden resulting from the care for the Apostle's material needs. This is confirmed by the fact that, in his other letter to the same community and in the context of warning them against idleness (II Thess. 3:6-15), the same Paul says: "For you yourselves know how you ought to imitate us; we were not idle when we were with you, we did not eat any one's bread without paying, *but with toil and labor we worked night and day, that we might not burden any of you*" (vv.7-8).

But if we opt for this meaning of ἐν βάρει εἶναι, it remains for us to show that Paul's apostleship of Christ— ὡς Χριστοῦ ἀπόστολοι—gives him the possibility and right—δυνάμενοι—to require, or at least request, that the faithful take care of his material needs during his stay with them. Now a clear-cut proof for this right we find in the lengthy passage in I Cor. 9:1-15 where we read: "*Do we not have the right* to our food and drink? Do *we not have the right* to be accompanied by a wife, *as the other apostles?* ... Or is it only Barnabas and I *who have no right to refrain from working for a living?* ... If we have sown spiritual good among you, is it too much if we reap your material benefits? ...*" (vv.4-5, 6, 11). We will limit ourselves here to concluding from this text that apostleship gave to its bearer a right regarding his material needs. How widespread this tradition was in the early church is shown from the *Didache* (*The Teaching of the Twelve Apostles*):[15] "Now concerning the apostles and prophets. Act in accordance with the precept of the gospel. Every apostle—ἀπόστολος— who comes to you should be received as the Lord ... And when the apostles departs, he should receive nothing but bread until he finds his next lodging" (*Did.* 11:3-4, 6).

All the preceding shows that the Apostle Paul's intention in writing δυνάμενοι ἐν βάρει εἶναι is to require the Thessalonians to take care of his food and drink. What about our translation then: "though we might have made our importance felt"? We have preferred this translation for the following reasons:

(a) The right for someone to "show weight" to the others results from one's apostleship and not the other way around. In other words, "material weight" is the result of "spiritual weight"; (b) the idea in vv.6-7 is that as apostle, Paul is not seeking "honor and glorification—δόξαν" from men. These two reasons are enough in our eyes to justify the translation of ἐν βάρει εἶναι in conjunction with δόξαν.

Regarding the expression "as apostles of Christ—ὡς Χριστοῦ ἀπόστολοι" we would like to draw attention to the fact that this is the only instance where the word "apostle" appears in either of the epistles to the Thessalonians. As for its simple use without any comment—especially seeing that Paul did not introduce himself as apostle at the beginning of the letter—it shows two things: on the one hand, Paul was fully aware of the truth of his apostleship right from the start of his missionary activity; on the other, this apostleship was not heavily under question in Thessalonica. Now apostleship has always its source in Christ, as it is often stressed in the Pauline writings: Rom. 1:1, 5; I Cor. 1:1, 17; II Cor. 1:1; 11:13; Gal. 1:1; Eph. 1:1; 4:11; Col. 1:1. Yet Paul did not use his title for personal purposes—

---

[15] A Chrisian writing of the first half of the second century A.D.

although he had all the right to do so—but was "gentle—
ἤπιος" in the midst of the Thessalonians.

One would logically expect here that Paul would expand
immediately on this idea—he will actually do so in v.9 regarding v.7a, and in v.11 regarding v.7b. Yet his emphasis
on his extremely affectionate behavior toward the Thessalonians pushed him to open a bracket and make a general
statement that sheds considerable light on the psychology
of the missionary Paul as well as on his understanding of
his missionary work.

7c8. ὡς ἐὰν τροφὸς θάλπῃ τὰ ἑαυτῆς
τέκνα, οὕτως ὁμειρόμενοι ὑμῶν εὐδοκοῦμεν μεταδοῦναι ὑμῖν οὐ μόνον τὸ εὐαγγέλιον τοῦ Θεοῦ ἀλλὰ
καὶ τὰς ἑαυτῶν ψυχάς,

As a nurse takes care of her children, so—being
affectionately desirous of you—we see it well
pleasing to offer you not only the gospel of
God but even our own selves, because you became beloved to us.

We have said earlier that this sentence is a general statement
made by way of parenthesis. To be sure, in the passage 2:1-12 Paul
reminds the Thessalonians of all that has happened since he came
to evangelize them. It is then understandable that he uses his verbs
in the aorist. However, the main verb of vv.7c-8 "εὐδοκοῦμεν—
we see it well-pleasing" is strikingly in the present indicative.

Though the Apostle uses the image of fatherhood to
denote usually his love for the faithful he has evangelized—

and though this image does come up in this context (see
v.11)—still his extreme care for the Thessalonians could
not but reflect itself in this his letter written from a distance
while he was worrying about them. He is, as it were, overtaken at that point by the image of a nurse holding tightly
her *own* children (and not someone else's: τὰ ἑαυτῆς τέκνα) in order to bestow on them warmth and affection. Thus
Paul's caring embrace for the Thessalonians went to the
extent of giving himself along with the gospel. As to the
reason for this unlimited affection, it is that the believers in
the capital of Macedonia became beloved/dear to the Apostle,
which means that this bond of love was not an outcome of
their sonship to him—they were definitely not his own!—
but rather the latter was the result of the former. What might
this love be and mean?

First of all we should notice that Paul did not say: "because you became *so/to that extent* dear to us," *i.e.*, he did
not explain his care for the Thessalonians on the basis of a
love that was already there and has attained a peak in the
Apostle's life. He simply said: "because you became beloved
to us," *i.e.*, they were not beloved before and at some point
they became so for him. Our understanding of this verse is
thus linked to the meaning of "beloved—ἀγαπητοί." Now,
in the Pauline letters this word is said only of the believers.
Consequently the relation of love mentioned in our verse
results from the new situation the Thessalonians are in for
Paul, namely that they became of the "brethren—ἀδελφοί."
Moreover, the verb "you became—ἐγενήθητε" in the whole
epistle (1:5, 6; 2:5, 7, 10, 14) always refers to a specific
past event, namely Paul's preaching to the Thessalonians
as well as their acceptance of the faith at his hands. This
further explains why the Apostle did not simply write: "So
we were ready to offer you our own selves"—which would
have been only logical if the bond of love between them
was simply a human one with no reference to their faith—
but he specifically said: "So we see it well pleasing to offer

you *not only the gospel of God* but even our own selves."

All of the above is a clear indication that only the gospel of God is the basis for relations between an apostle and those whom he evangelizes. However, this gospel is a living reality and the apostle is fully aware that the extent of his success in his conveying it to the others is conditioned by the extent in which this gospel—God's gospel—becomes his own as apostle (see 1:5 and our comments there). In other words, the welding that arises between the message and its bearer makes out of the apostle's self a vessel for the gospel; now, this vessel might become a hindrance if it were not up to the level of the exhausting love required by the contained treasure (see especially II Cor. 4:7-12).

v.9. μνημονεύετε γάρ, ἀδελφοί, τὸν κόπον ἡμῶν καὶ τὸν μόχθον· νυκτὸς
καὶ ἡμέρας ἐργαζόμενοι πρὸς τὸ
μὴ ἐπιβαρῆσαί τινα ὑμῶν ἐκηρύξαμεν εἰς ὑμᾶς τὸ εὐαγγέλιον τοῦ
Θεοῦ.

For you remember our labor and toil, brethren: while we were working night and day—that we might not burden any of you—we proclaimed to you the gospel of God.

After the parenthesis in vv.7c-8 the Apostle resumes his main thought, rendering in detail in the following verses what he has briefly put in v.7a-b. As for our verse, it is an explanation of v.7a: "though we might have made felt our importance as apostles of Christ." Here Paul mentions the labor and toil—κόπον καὶ μόχθον—which he showed in Thessalonica as a proof for his not having exercised his apostolic right. The words κόπος and μόχθος reflect the same idea: tiring work and exhausting labor; however, each stresses a specific aspect. Κόπος has the meaning of the work or labor itself, whereas μόχθος carries rather that of the weariness and exhaustion resulting from such work or labor. This explains why, whereas κόπος appears many times in the Pauline letters as well as in the other New Testament books, μόχθος is mentioned only thrice, by Paul, and always along with κόπος (II Cor. 11:27; I Thess. 2:9; II Thess. 3:8). In all of these three last instances it is obvious from the context that Paul's intention is to underline the physical exhaustion resulting from his labor. In our verse here, the Apostle himself actually explains what he means by these two words: he and his companions performed manual labor[16] that assured them livelihood in order not to burden any of the Thessalonians.

However, Paul knows only too well that the issue at stake here is not his manual labor in itself, but rather his labor as Christ's apostle, since it is his right not to have to worry about working for his livelihood while he is acting as missionary. Therefore, when asking the Thessalonians to remember his behavior in their midst, his wording is the following: "night and day working—ἐργαζόμενοι—in order not to burden any of you, we preached—ἐκηρύξαμεν—to you the gospel of God." The idea of preaching took over the main verb κηρύσσω, which appears in the aorist (i.e., in the same tense as the verb γίγνομαι—to be, to behave),[17] whereas the mention of manual labor is only secondarily mentioned in the participle ἐργαζόμενοι. Paul, as it were,

---

[16]The verb ἐργάζομαι carries the meaning of manual work. See Rom. 4:4-5; I Cor. 4:12; 9:6; Eph. 4:28; Col. 3:23; I Thess. 4:11; II Thess. 3:10-12.

[17]Ἐγενήθημεν in 1:5; 2:5, 7, 10. See also "what an entrance/welcome we had—ὁποίαν εἴσοδον ἔσχομεν" (1:9).

was reminding them not so much of his manual work as
such, but rather of his doing an *extra* and *exhausting* labor
while he was performing his main assignment: the preaching
of God's gospel.

Paul uses two verbs to refer to his missionary work: εὐαγγελίζομαι to evangelize, to carry the gospel (deriving from the noun
εὐαγγέλιον—gospel) and κηρύσσω—to proclaim, to herald. The
former underlines the notion of the gospel message carried by the
apostle, while the latter emphasizes the action of preaching itself in
that the first meaning of the verb κηρύσσω is the declaration in a
loud voice done by the κῆρυξ—herald.

v.10. ὑμεῖς μάρτυρες καὶ ὁ Θεός, ὡς
ὁσίως καὶ δικαίως καὶ ἀμέμπτως
ὑμῖν τοῖς πιστεύουσιν ἐγενήθημεν,

You are witnesses, and God also, how holy
and righteous and blameless was our behavior
to you believers;

Manual work is external and tangible; thus the Apostle
found it enough to refer to the Thessalonians' memory to
prove his point. Here, however, Paul is talking about inner
matters; thus he is obliged to appeal to their *witness*. He
even calls on God Himself to bear witness, since He alone
is able to decide in such matters as holiness, righteousness
and blameless behavior.

The adverb ὁσίως carries the meaning of holiness and
purity, however, not in its general understanding as does
the word ἅγιος, but rather in its liturgical connotation.
Sure enough, the adjective ὅσιος in the Old Testament is

usually found in conjunction with the sacrificial worship at
the Temple.[18] This shows that Paul was fully aware that his
preaching activity was a kind of righteous and acceptable
sacrifice offered to God. Although ὁσίως appears only here
in reference to the Apostle's preaching, the same idea is
nevertheless clearly found in Phil. 2:16-17 and Rom. 15:16.
The first passage reads thus: "... holding fast the word of
life, so that in the day of Christ I may be proud that I did
not run in vain or labor in vain. Even if I am to be poured
as a libation—σπένδομαι—upon the sacrifice—θυσίᾳ—and
liturgical service—λειτουργίᾳ[19]—of your faith, I am glad
and rejoice with you all" (Phil. 2:16-17). The running and
labor of v.16 are undoubtedly Paul's missionary activity (see
I Thess. 2:1 and especially 3:5). Yet the Apostle clarifies
in v.17 that this his work is like a sacrifice—θυσία—resulting from the liturgy—λειτουργία—which he is performing
in order to present the Philippians' faith as a libation/
offering to God. In other words, he sees himself as a priest
serving the altar of the Most High and offering Him the
faith of the Gentiles as a good and acceptable sacrifice.
Even more: he considers the success of his mission a libation being burnt together with the sacrifice.

In Rom. 15:16 Paul writes: "... to be a minister—
λειτουργόν—of Christ Jesus to the Gentiles in the priestly
service—ἱερουργοῦντα—of the gospel of God, so that the
offering—ἡ προσφορά—of the Gentiles may be acceptable,
sanctified by the Holy Spirit." Here again it is clear that
the Apostle considers himself a priest of Christ to the Gentiles
as fulfilling the ministry of preaching God's gospel and
endeavoring that they become an acceptable offering to God,
acceptable because it is sanctified by the power of the Holy
Spirit, i.e., in baptism. Elsewhere in his letter to the Romans

---

[18]This is clearly reflected in the following New Testament passages:
Lk. 1:73-75; Heb. 7:26; I Tim. 2:8; Tit. 1:8.
[19]The word λειτουργία refers specifically to the priestly ministry at
the temple.

he sees himself as an oblation, considering the afflictions, persecutions, hunger and dangers that befall him during his performing of his missionary duty a sacrifice offered to God: "Who shall separate us from the love of Christ? Shall tribulation, or distress, or persecution, or famine, or nakedness, or peril, or sword? As it is written, 'For thy sake we are being killed all the day long; we are regarded as *sheep to be slaugtered*' " (8:35-36).

Our conclusion is that Paul saw his apostolic activity as a priestly ministry, while the faith of the Gentiles was for him a sacrifice acceptable to God. Moreover the Apostle considered this ministry itself a libation poured over the sacrifice. Thus the term ὁσίως has both meanings.

Yet there is in the Old Testament another essential aspect in the life of the children of that Testament. Besides offering sacrifices in the Temple they were to keep God's Law; thus, righteousness in their eyes consisted in keeping the Law's commandments. And Paul, himself an ex-Pharisee, gave great importance to the issue of the Old Testament law (see the Epistle to the Romans); that is why he took God as witness that his behavior among the Thessalonians had been righteous—δικαίως, *i.e.*, according to God's law.

As for the adverb ἀμέμπτως, it carries the other face of the meaning of δικαίως, namely that the Apostle's righteousness regarding the law made him blameless in its eyes. But why did Paul use ἀμέμπτως along with δικαίως, whereas he mentioned only ὁσίως regarding the temple ministry? The reason is that "blameless—ἀμέμπτως" is in direct relation to the idea of judgment before God's tribunal at the second coming (see 3:13 and 5:23); thus, in his use of the adverbs ὁσίως, δικαίως and ἀμέμπτως, he saw himself fulfilling his apostolic office on three levels: as a priest performing his ministry at God's altar in all holiness, as a righteous man keeping all the commandments of the law, and consequently blameless on the dread judgment day.

The use of ἀμέμπτως along with ὁσίως and δικαίως confirms once more that Paul's main concern during the writing of this letter is the subject of the Lord's coming again (see our comments on 1:3).

Now Paul adhered strictly to this behavior, which requires an unimaginable spiritual struggle, for the sake of the faithful in Thessalonica, so that he would not be an issue of scandal for them but rather a reason for their continuous advancement in the saving faith. That explains his deep hurt as well as his bitter apologia when he heard that there were some accusations against his behavior in Thessalonica (see 2:3, 5-6).

Once more we are confronted with the reality that conveying the gospel is influenced by the person and conduct of its bearer.

vv.11-12. καθάπερ οἴδατε ὡς ἕνα ἕκαστον ὑμῶν ὡς πατὴρ τέκνα ἑαυτοῦ παρακαλοῦντες ὑμᾶς καὶ παραμυθούμενοι καὶ μαρτυρόμενοι εἰς τὸ περιπατεῖν ὑμᾶς ἀξίως τοῦ Θεοῦ τοῦ καλοῦντος ὑμᾶς εἰς τὴν ἑαυτοῦ βασιλείαν καὶ δόξαν.

For you know how, like a father with his children, we exhorted each one of you and encouraged you and charged you to lead a life worthy of God who calls you in His own kingdom and glory.

After taking God as witness for his performing his duty

in all holiness, righteousness and without blame, Paul returns once more to the Thessalonians' memory in saying:
"as you know—καθάπερ οἴδατε." With this expression he
starts vv.11 and 12, where he intends to justify his statement
in v.7b that he conducted himself in all gentleness in their
midst. For this he uses the picture of an over-affectionate
father, one of his dearest images, to express his relationship
with those who believed through him (I Cor. 4:14-17; II Cor.
6:13; Gal. 4:19; Phil. 2:22; Philem. 10).

The Greek pronoun ἕκαστος (ἕκαστον in the accusative) means
each of many (more than two) and is used alone. Thus the mention
of εἷς (ἕνα in the accusative)—which means one—before ἕκαστον
is a powerful indication as to how much the Apostle wanted to
stress the idea of his care for the Thessalonians *one by one*.

As for the use of τέκνα ἑαυτοῦ (a reflexive indicating emphasis)
instead of τέκνα αὐτοῦ after πατήρ, it is explained by the influence
of τὰ ἑαυτῆς τέκνα in v.7, which shows the intensity of Paul's feeling
of paternity toward the faithful of Thessalonica.

Whereas in v.11 the Apostle clarified the *how*—the aspect—of his activity in Thessalonica, in v.12 he reminds the
faithful there of the *what*—the content—of such activity,
which he epitomizes in the following three participles:
exhorting—παρακαλοῦντες, encouraging—παραμυθούμενοι, charging/asking—μαρτυρόμενοι.

The verb παρακαλέω with Paul usually has the meaning
of exhortation resulting from preaching and guidance, an
exhortation that pushes the faithful to fulfill the Apostle's
demands on them; hence the frequent use of this verb in the
Pauline writings.

We find the verb παραμυθέομαι only three times in
Paul's letters, two of which together with the verb παρακαλέω (here and in I Cor. 14:3); as for the noun παρα-
μύθιον, it is used once and in parallel with the noun
παράκλησις (Phil. 2:1). They have the connotation of
encouragement. This is confirmed by I Thess. 5:14 where

the verb appears in the following context: "and we exhort you, brethren; admonish the idle, *encourage*—παραμυθεῖ-σϑε—*the fainthearted, help the weak, be patient with all.*"[20]

Finally the verb μαρτύρομαι has the meaning of making the faithful take an oath before God with the intention of urging them to do that which the Apostle is asking of them, namely to lead a life worthy of God.

The verb "περιπατέω—to walk" of v.12 with Paul always has the meaning of conducting oneself. This results from the fact that it is the translation of the Hebrew verb *halak*, which reflects both meanings: the proper one of walking, as well as the figurative one of conducting oneself.

Now, if we remember that the Apostle Paul used to be a Pharisee, then it will be easy for us to understand the reason behind the frequent use of the verb περιπατέω in his letters, and always in the meaning of spiritual conduct. The teachings of the Pharisees were of two essential kinds: the *halākāh* and the *haggādāh*. The first kind embraced all the teachings and interpretations referring to the *torāh* or law, that is the five books of Moses (Genesis, Exodus, Leviticus, Numbers and Deuteronomy). The *torāh* or law represents the basic part of the Old Testament in the Judaic tradition, since it comprises God's commandments that govern religious, social as well as personal life. Hence, the explanations given these commandments were known under the name *halākāh*, meaning the conduct or way of life which a Jew is to follow. Consequently the teachings of the *halākāh* are necessary for him and he must practice them, since in doing that he will have fulfilled the commandments of the law.

As for the *haggādāh*[21] or oral tradition, it comprises teachings and interpretations resulting from the study of all the other Old Testament texts: the historical, prophetic, didactic and poetical books. The content of the *haggādāh* is a kind of preaching, exhortation and guidance to emulate the lives of the righteous and to follow their teachings as they appear in those books. Therefore, it is not on the doctrinal level of the *halākāh*.

---

[20]See also Jn. 11:19 and 31 where the meaning is the encouragement resulting from comfort received in affliction.

[21]From the Hebrew verb *higgîd* which means: to tell, to relate.

All of the aforementioned indicates that Paul's teachings and living accordingly are in his eyes on the same level as that of the *halākāh*, that is on a doctrinal level of utmost importance. In other words, the conduct or way of life according to the Apostle's teaching is both essential and necessary, and it is impossible that someone be a believer without it. Consequently one might say: Christian conduct is not a matter of choice for a believer, but rather an essential factor in his being Christian.

Now, such a conduct is to be "worthy of God," *i.e.*, worthy of His approval and favor. In order that our way of life be of such a quality, we will have to remember that it is after all an outcome of God's calling us and thus a response to this call. God is the one who calls (see also I Thess. 5:24; Rom. 9:12; Gal. 5:8), that is the first cause for this new status which qualifies us as believers. Hence, He is the one to decide the level of our answering His call as well as the worthiness of such an answer.

Since the participle in Greek can appear in any of four tenses: present, future, aorist and perfect,[22] we can imagine the array of possibilities out of which someone writing in Greek may choose in order to render accurately his thought. Thus, if Paul wanted to underline the instant of the call, that is the fact of the calling itself which God extended to the Thessalonians through the Apostle, he would have used the aorist participle: "τοῦ καλέσαντος—who called."[23] But the use of the present participle (τοῦ καλοῦντος—who calls) is intended, since he wants to say that God is the one who calls (in an absolute way), and the church—the community of believers—is formed around His call and out of it.[24] In other words, the expression "who calls" is a kind of definition of God. Indeed Paul could have as well dismissed the word "God" and simply said: "... to lead a life worthy of Him who calls you...." This our conclusion is confirmed by I Thess. 5:24: "Faithful is He who calls you—πιστὸς ὁ καλῶν ὑμᾶς," as well as by Gal. 5:8: "This persua-

---

[22]The last three are usually translated into English periphrastically by using a personal and/or relative pronoun followed by the verb.

[23]See Gal. 1:6.

[24]Notice that the noun "ἐκκλησία—church" derives from the verb "καλέω—to call."

sion is not from Him who called you—ἡ πεισμονὴ οὐκ ἐκ τοῦ καλοῦντος ὑμᾶς." Indeed, in Rom. 9:12 we find the expression "the one who calls" in its absolute form without object complement: "... not because of works, but because of the one who calls—οὐκ ἐξ ἔργων, ἀλλ' ἐκ τοῦ καλοῦντος."

At this point we may justify our preference for the reading τοῦ καλοῦντος (who calls) over τοῦ καλέσαντος (who called) which appears in two main manuscripts "Codex Sinaiticus" and A. As we have seen, Paul uses usually ὁ καλῶν (see Rom. 9:12; Gal. 5:8 and especially I Thess. 5:24 in our epistle). The only exception is Gal. 1:6: "I am astonished that you are so quickly deserting him who called you—τοῦ καλέσαντος ὑμᾶς—in the grace of Christ, for another gospel." We believe that τοῦ καλέσαντος appears in this case because the Apostle was defining the way the call took place (in the grace of Christ); thus he was referring to its happening at a particular point in the past, namely when the Galatians accepted the faith at his hands and were baptized. We find confirmation for our opinion in that later in the same letter (Gal. 5:8) Paul comes back to the usual "τοῦ καλοῦντος ὑμᾶς—who calls you."

Now the call God extends to us is to/toward/into His own kingdom and glory. God's kingdom, or rather kingship, is where He reigns absolutely and everything happens according to His will: "... Thy kingdom come, Thy will be done on earth as it is in heaven." Our entrance in the kingdom means therefore that we put ourselves under God's aegis and consider Him the first and last criterion for the correctness of our thinking, attitudes and actions. Now that does not happen in fact unless we are in God's presence; hence, the Apostle completed his saying about the kingdom with the word "δόξα—glory." He is saying, as it were, that the entrance into the kingdom is actually entrance into glory. What might this glory be?

To grasp as fully as possible the meaning of this word would require extensive research and an independent detailed study. Therefore we shall limit ourselves to the following clarification. In the book of Exodus we read that the Lord said to Moses: "Speak to the people of Israel that they take for me an offering... *And let them make me a sanctuary that I may dwell in their midst*" (25:2, 8). After the work was completed (40:33) "*the cloud covered the tent of meet-*

ing, and the glory of the Lord filled the tabernacle. And Moses was not able to enter the tent of meeting, because the cloud abode upon it, *and the glory of the Lord filled the tabernacle"* (40:34-35). This means that the Lord comes in His glory, *i.e.*, makes Himself present among us in His glory. In other words, God's glory is God Himself in His movement toward man, that is the face with which He shines to mankind, since we are unable to behold God in His essence but only inasmuch as He appears and reveals Himself to us.

Thus the descent (abiding) of God's glory on (in) the holy sanctuary under the aspect of a cloud means the descent (abiding) of God Himself there. This is precisely what results from the following text taken out of the same book: "Then Moses went up on the mountain, and the cloud covered the mountain. *The glory of the Lord* settled on Mount Sinai, and the cloud covered it six days; and on the seventh day *he called to Moses out of the midst of the cloud.* Now the appearance of *the glory of the Lord* was like a devouring fire on the top of the mountain in the sight of the people of Israel. *And Moses entered the cloud,* and went up on the mountain. And Moses was on the mountain forty days and forty nights" (24:15-18).

Similarly, after the building of the Jerusalem temple in the days of King Solomon, we read: "And when the priests came out of the holy place, *a cloud filled the house of the Lord,* so that the priests could not stand to minister because of the cloud; for *the glory of the Lord filled the house of the Lord.* Then Solomon said: *The Lord* has set the sun in the heavens, but *has said that He would dwell in thick darkness.* I have built *Thee* an exalted house, a place *for Thee to dwell in* forever" (I Kg. 8:10-13).

Finally in the book of Ezekiel we find the following: "Afterward he brought me to the gate, the gate facing east. And behold, *the glory of the God of Israel came* from the east; and the sound of his coming was like the sound of many waters; and the earth shone with his *glory . . . As the glory of God entered the temple* by the gate facing east, the Spirit lifted me up, and brought me into the inner court; and behold, *the glory of the Lord filled the temple ... I heard one speaking to me out of the temple"* (43:1-6).

All these texts show that the glory of God is nothing but God's moving toward us. Hence, the entrance into God's kingdom, sharing in His life and being united to Him ... all these mean practically our entrance into His glory, and thus our glorification, that is, our sharing in that glory which deifies us. "And we all, with unveiled face, *beholding the glory of the Lord, are being changed into his likeness* from one degree of glory to another; for this comes from the Lord who is the Spirit" (II Cor. 3:18). As for this change/ transformation, it is realized in Christ Jesus as we read later in the same epistle: "For it is the God who said: Let light shine out of darkness; who has shone in our hearts to give the light of *the knowledge of the glory of God in the face of Christ"* (4:6).

The above study explains why in Paul's eyes the glory, that is our glorification through our sharing in God's glory, is the ultimate goal of God's calling to us. "... And those whom he predestined *He also called*; and those whom He called He also justified; and those whom He justified *He also glorified"* (Rom. 8:30); "... in order to *make known the riches of His glory* for the vessels of mercy, *which He has prepared beforehand for glory*, even us *whom He has called*, not from the Jews only but also from the Gentiles" (Rom. 9:23-24). And what is the ultimate goal if not the inheritance which God prepared for the saints, that is the believers in Jesus Christ: "... that the God of our Lord Jesus Christ, *the Father of glory*, may give you a spirit of wisdom and of revelation in the knowledge of Him, having the eyes of your hearts enlightened that you may know what is *the hope to which He has called you*, what are the *riches of His glorious inheritance* in the saints ..." (Eph. 1:17-18) ?

v.13. Καὶ διὰ τοῦτο καὶ ἡμεῖς εὐχαριστοῦμεν τῷ Θεῷ ἀδιαλείπτως, ὅτι
παραλαβόντες λόγον ἀκοῆς παρ'
ἡμῶν Θεοῦ ἐδέξασθε οὐ λόγον
ἀνθρώπων ἀλλὰ καθὼς ἀληθῶς
ἐστιν λόγον Θεοῦ, ὃς καὶ ἐνεργεῖται ἐν ὑμῖν τοῖς πιστεύουσιν.

And we also thank God constantly for this,
that when you received the word of God
which you heard from us, you accepted it not
as the word of men, but as it really is, the
word of God, which is at work in you believers.

Finally the Apostle reminds the Thessalonians anew that
he is constantly—ἀδιαλείπτως—thanking God because they
have accepted the word of the gospel which he and his
companions brought them. But the unique feature of this
verse is that it gives us in detail an idea about the different
stages that bring about the acceptance of the gospel. We
shall try now to clarify these stages as well as their importance.

Undoubtedly the starting point is "the word—λόγον"
which, as we have shown in 1:6, signifies the gospel. But
here Paul qualifies "the word" as being "a word of hearing—
λόγον ἀκοῆς," an expression found only here in the whole
New Testament. It means that the Thessalonians heard the
gospel at the hand of the Apostle, as it appears from the
immediately following "παρ' ἡμῶν—from us," since the
preposition παρά—when governing a genitive—means from,
from the side of, from the part of. To be convinced of the

importance of the idea of hearing in matter of conveying the
gospel, see also Rom. 10:8-17; Gal. 3:2, 5; Col. 1:6, 23.
This means that the content of the gospel transmitted by the
tongue is what saves, if the person believes. And Paul is
fully aware of this reality; therefore, after emphasizing the
hearing in the transmission of the gospel, indeed after having defined the latter as "word of hearing," he immediately
introduces the other two distinguishing attributes of "the
word," namely: that it is coming from the Apostle's lips
(παρ' ἡμῶν—from us) and that it is God's (τοῦ Θεοῦ).

The close interrelation in Paul's mind between these three attributes of the
gospel—that it is a heard word, a word uttered by an apostle, and the word
of God—cannot explain the heavy syntax in the original Greek: παραλαβόντες λόγον ἀκοῆς παρ' ἡμῶν τοῦ Θεοῦ. Here the noun λόγον
has two genitives, ἀκοῆς and τοῦ Θεοῦ not linked by the conjunction καί;
the second genitive τοῦ Θεοῦ is even separated from λόγου by the expression παρ' ἡμῶν. Paul could very well have written: παραλαβόντες
(τὸν) λόγον (τοῦ) Θεοῦ ὃν παρ' ἡμῶν ἠκούσατε.[25] Therefore, the
only plausible explanation is that what he has actually written carries a
logical sequence having to do with reality. That which the Thessalonians
received was a word they heard, and, although its bearers were human
beings, it was God's; or in other words, that which was heard came from the
apostles, but its source was God. If then παρ' ἡμῶν was mentioned
before τοῦ Θεοῦ, it is because it logically follows ἀκοῆς: you heard from
us.

There lies precisely the delicate but essential point in the
transmission of the message of salvation: in that it is the
word of God and a word delivered by human beings *at
the same time*. Put otherwise: *who* is heard are the apostles
and *what* is heard is the word of God. This explains why,
in Paul's eyes, the stage of evangelization (which comes first)
is followed by two others, and not only one, both taking place
at the level of the hearers: First, the *reception, i.e.,* taking
note of—as well as into consideration—what is said; second,
its acceptance and welcome as it really is: God's word.
Speaking of the first step Paul uses the verb παραλαμβάνω, meaning: to take from, to receive . . . , which indicates

[25]Which is actually how the RSV text reads.

an action not requiring a positive step or a participation or a decision on the part of the one taking it. That is what differentiates it from the verb δέχομαι.

Nevertheless παραλαμβάνω has a special connotation when used by Paul in conjunction with the gospel, since it carries then the idea of receiving a tradition or a traditional teaching, and consequently it underlines that the gospel and the transmitted teachings do not originate with the bearer, but rather have their prime source in the Lord Jesus or his twelve apostles. This is reflected in the use of παραλαμβάνω together with the verb παραδίδωμι—to deliver, to transmit where we clearly have the concept of transmission and reception, that is tradition.[26] The two verbs παραλαμβάνω and παραδίδωμι are thus connected in a continuous succession leading up to the source: Jesus Christ or his twelve apostles. This last point explains by the way why Paul applies to himself the verb παραλαμβάνω: "For I received—παρέλαβον—from the Lord what I also delivered—παρέδωκα—to you ..." (I Cor. 11:23); "For I delivered—παρέδωκα—to you as of first importance what I also received—παρέλαβον ..." (I Cor. 15:3); "For I did not receive—παρέλαβον—it (*viz.* the gospel) from man ..." (Gal. 1:12). All of the above indicates that what the Thessalonians received was the same gospel and teaching found in all the churches.

But to receive the gospel is not enough. Those who receive it are asked to welcome it and accept it as being the word of God. Hence the main verb in our verse is not παραλαμβάνω (which appears as an aorist participle whose translation is: when or after you received), but rather "ἐδέξασθε—you accepted" from the verb δέχομαι, meaning: to accept, to take approving of, to welcome. Thus the actual reason for the constant prayer of thanksgiving to God is not that the Thessalonians have merely taken notice of the gospel, but that they accepted Paul's preaching for what it really is: the word of God and not a human one.

There remains, however, the big question: how does this

---

[26]See II Thess. 3:6.

transition from the stage of reception (παραλαμβάνω) to that of welcome and acceptance (δέχομαι) happen in practice? What does actually push the receivers or hearers of the apostles' word, that is a human word, into accepting it as the word of God? How does the hearer of the apostles gain the assurance that what these men are uttering is indeed God's word and not the word of men, as Paul puts it? The only possible answer is: it is faith resulting from the effectiveness of the divine word. This is actually what we read at the end of the verse: "... which is (still) at work— ὅς καὶ ἐνεργεῖται—in you believers." God's word works— is active—in the believers, and could it yield anything else besides that which brings them salvation (see I Cor. 1:18; Eph. 1:13; I Thess. 2:16; II Thess. 2:13-14)? And what could bring them salvation except faith (see Rom. 1:16; I Cor. 1:21; 15:2; Eph. 2:8, *Phil. 1:27-28*; II Thess. 2:13-14)? Now, if God's word is *still* at work and enhances faith in the hearts of the Thessalonians, it is only obvious that God's word itself is also that which has produced that faith, *i.e.*, planted it, in them when they first heard the Apostle's gospel.

However, this does not mean at all that the phenomenon, or rather event, of faith takes place in the Thessalonians' hearts *in whatever manner* the evangelization might have happened. No! The apostle may not forget that *his words* form the link, are actually the meeting point of the hearer with God's word. Thus it is incumbent upon him to put all possible and impossible effort to make out of the word heard from *him* (παρ' ἡμῶν) the word of God (τοῦ Θεοῦ) to its utmost extent. In other words, the evangelizer must always try to arrive at the point where he can say that his gospel is God's gospel (see our comments on the word "gospel" in 1:5); otherwise he might become an obstacle between man and God, and consequently unfaithful to that which he has been entrusted with (see 2:4). The apostle's duty is to render the phenomenon/event of faith for men plausible, not impossible.

Paul ends the verse by saying that the word of God is still at work in the Thessalonians, which shows that one of the believer's duties is to persevere in a continuous intercourse with God's word, since it alone guarantees the growth of his faith that brings him salvation.

v.14. ὑμεῖς γὰρ μιμηταὶ ἐγενήθητε, ἀ-δελφοί, τῶν ἐκκλησιῶν τοῦ Θεοῦ τῶν οὐσῶν ἐν τῇ Ἰουδαίᾳ ἐν Χρι-στῷ Ἰησοῦ, ὅτι τὰ αὐτὰ ἐπάθετε καὶ ὑμεῖς ὑπὸ τῶν ἰδίων συμφυ-λετῶν, καθὼς καὶ αὐτοὶ ὑπὸ τῶν Ἰουδαίων,

For you, brethren, became imitators of the churches of God in Christ Jesus, which are in Judea; for you suffered the same things from your countrymen as they did from the Jews.

The faith of the Thessalonians—or rather the effectiveness of God's word in them as believers—shows in their sufferings for the sake of their new faith. Paul sees in this a comparison to the churches of Judea. But why specifically these churches? We believe that there are two reasons for that: (a) the close similarity resulting from the fact that, in both cases, the persecution was an action undertaken by kinsmen of the recent believers (the Jews in Judea and the

Thessalonians in the Macedonian capital); (b) the Jews of
Thessalonica were behind the persecution of the Thessalonian
Christians as we read in Acts 17:1-9, 13 (see also our com-
ments on 2:3, 5).

To make sure that he is intending the Christian communities in Judea, Paul clarifies by saying: "the churches
that are in Christ Jesus," since this is the new definition
which differentiates the Christian churches from the Jewish
synagogues. The multiplicity of the Christian communities in
the Judean region resulted from the scattering of the faithful from Jerusalem thither due to a great persecution that
fell over that city (Acts 8:1-3 and 9:1). As for the use of
the plural "churches—τῶν ἐκκλησιῶν," it indicates that
each city or cluster of adjacent villages formed an independent
church. That seems to be the custom followed in those days
even in Judea itself where Jerusalem was the capital and
where it would have been quite easy that all Christian
communities there be considered one church gathered around
the holy city.[27] Nonetheless, the concept of extreme centralism
did not occur in the minds of first-century Christians.

Now, the similarity between the church of the Thessalonians
and those in Judea has two aspects: (a) the Thessalonians
suffered (ἐπάθετε) the same sufferings—τὰ αὐτά—which
the faithful of Judea endured; (b) in both cases the per-
secutors were kinsmen, as mentioned above.

Though Paul uses in 1:6 the word "affliction—θλῖψις"
to refer to the distresses suffered by the Thessalonians who
thus became imitators of the Lord and himself, he clearly
says here that those afflictions and difficulties were actually
physical sufferings as a result of persecution. Indeed the
intent behind the use of the verb "ἐπάθετε—you suffered"
is obviously physical pain for the following two reasons:
(a) the verb "πάσχω[28]—to suffer" usually in Greek and

---

[27]See our comments on 1:1 about the importance of Jerusalem and the
church there.

[28]Ἐπάθατε is in the aorist and thus refers to a given past event.

always in Paul means: to be in pain, to undergo physical suffering; (b) the use of the expression "τὰ αὐτά—the same things" reflects the absolute resemblance between the two events. And we do know from the Book of Acts what the Christians suffered in Jerusalem (5:24; 7:58; 8:1-3; 26:10) as well as in the rest of Judea (9:13; 26:11).

v.15. τῶν καὶ τὸν κύριον ἀποκτεινάντων Ἰησοῦν καὶ τοὺς προφήτας, καὶ ἡμᾶς ἐκδιωξάντων, καὶ Θεῷ μὴ ἀρεσκόντων, καὶ πᾶσιν ἀνθρώποις ἐναντίων.

who killed both the Lord Jesus and the prophets, and drove us out, thus displeasing God and opposing all men,

However, the Apostle Paul immediately consoles the Thessalonians by stressing that both they and the churches of Judea are not the first to be persecuted. At this point his memory carries him back to what he and his companions had to suffer at the hands of the Jews. Yet, Christ and the prophets preceded everybody on that path.

Paul starts by stating that the Jews have killed the Lord Jesus as well as the prophets; in that, he agrees with what the early church taught through the apostles (Acts 2:23) and other church leaders (7:52). Thus the utmost sin committed by the Jews in the person of their leaders is that they killed Jesus of Nazareth, the Lord. Yet, this ultimate crime was but the last of a series of crimes perpetrated by the Jews against the prophets, *i.e.*, against those who carry

God's word and therefore against His representatives in Israel (see Mt. 21:33-46/Mk. 12:1-12/Lk. 20:9-19; Mt. 23:29-31/Lk. 11:47-48; Mt. 23:34-36/Lk. 11:49-51; Mt. 23:37/Lk. 13:34).

As the prophets were the bearers of God's word in the Old Testament, the apostles are the heralds of the saving gospel, *i.e.*, "the word—τὸν λόγον" (see 1:6) or "the word of the Lord—ὁ λόγος τοῦ κυρίου" (see 1:7), in the New Testament. Thus Paul emphasizes to the Thessalonians that the Jews were not satisfied with killing Jesus of Nazareth, but that they are persisting in their evil deed by persecuting His apostles who carry the good news of His resurrection from the dead as Lord.

The verb ἐκδιώκω is found only here in the New Testament. Indeed, like the other New Testament writers, Paul normally uses the verb διώκω and the noun διωγμός to render the notion of persecution. Why then ἐκδιώκω here? The reason, we believe, is that this verb expresses, besides the idea of persecution, that of "driving out" resulting from the prefix ἐκ. Thus, the Apostle might be referring to what happened to him in Thessalonica (Acts 17:10) and Beroea (17:14) as well as previously in Antioch of Pisidia (13:14, 50), Iconium (14:1, 5-6) and Lystra (14:6, 19-20).

Paul goes on to write that this action on the part of the Jews makes them displeasing to God as well as in opposition to all men. God's non-approval is due to the fact that, by persecuting the apostles, the Jews are trying to hinder the divine purpose of saving all people through the gospel (2:16; see also Rom. 1:16; 9:24; Gal. 6:15; Eph. 3:5-6). The Jews' enmity for all men on the other hand, results from two things: (a) if the gospel does not reach the Gentiles, these will remain far from God and thus non-participants in the salvation prepared for them in Jesus Christ; in other words, they will remain under the curse of sin and death (1:19; see also Rom. 1:18-32; 5:12-19; 6:20-23); (b) absence of faith in Jesus Christ maintains the wall of partition and

enmity between Jew and Gentile which results from the law
(Eph. 2:12-18); this wall seals, as it were, absolute dissension between circumcised and uncircumcised (Eph. 2:11),
whereas there is no basis for such dissension in Christ (Gal.
3:26-29; 6:15-16; Col. 3:9-11), since in Him all men become—through faith and baptism—Abraham's children (Rom.
4:18-25; Gal. 3:29), God's chosen ones, holy and beloved
(Col. 3:12), fellow citizens and members of God's household (Eph. 2:19).

We have considered the passage "and displeasing God and opposing all men" logically related to the preceding without giving
"καί—and" the value of a simple conjunction on the basis of the
following: (a) the expression "non-pleasing—μὴ ἀρεσκόντων"
is a (continuous) present participle and has thus the function of an
adjective, as is the case of its parallel word "ἐναντίων—opponents"
which is an adjective; (b) whereas "ἀποκτεινάντων—killed" and
"ἐκδιωξάντων—persecuted" are aorist participles and indicate therefore specific past actions.

v.16. κωλυόντων ἡμᾶς τοῖς ἔθνεσιν λαλῆσαι ἵνα σωθῶσιν, εἰς τὸ ἀνα-
πληρῶσαι αὐτῶν τὰς ἁμαρτίας
πάντοτε. Ἔφθασεν δὲ ἐπ᾽ αὐτοὺς
ἡ ὀργὴ εἰς τέλος.

by hindering us from speaking to the Gentiles
that they may be saved—so as to fill up the
measure of their sins always. God's wrath has
indeed come upon them until the end!

The use of the verb "κωλύω—to hinder" in the present

indicative on the one hand, and the absence of the conjunction "καί—and" before it on the other, clearly indicate
that the first part of this verse is an explanation of the immediately preceding: "thus displeasing God and opposing
all men."

It appears from our verse that the Jews' opposition to all
men and their displeasing God are not an immediate con-
sequence of their persecution of the apostles, but rather of
the fact that they thus hinder the apostles from carrying
the gospel to the Gentiles so that these might be saved.[29] The
magnitude of the Jews' sin in so doing lies in the fact that
the gospel brings salvation to those who receive it, *i.e.*, it
realizes the purpose (I Thess. 5:9; II Thess. 2:13) for which
God has sent His only-begotten Son (Rom. 5:6-11), be we
Jews or Gentiles. "For I am not ashamed of the gospel: it
is the power of God for salvation to every one who has
faith, to the Jew first and also to the Greek" (Rom. 1:16).

It seems then that the sins of the Jews against God's
will were piling up until the day when they went beyond
measure;[30] that is precisely what is meant by "filling up the
measure of sin." The adverb "always—πάντοτε" results from
the fact that the apostles' preaching of Jesus Christ is the
last essential stage in the life of the Jews regarding their
relation to God: with the gospel the last chance has gone
and their sins are fulfilled. Consequently, the time unfold-
ing after the appearance of Jesus Christ is a time of declaring
what the Lord Jesus has done "once and for all—ἐφάπαξ."[31]
As for the Jews' rejection of the apostles' preaching after
their rejection of the prophets and the Lord Jesus, it means
that this sin of rejection/refusal has been repeated "always—
πάντοτε," that is generation after generation until the fullness and completeness of salvation time in Jesus Christ.

---

[29]That the verb "καλέω—speak" refers to preaching the gospel has
been shown in our comments on 2:2 and 4.
[30]See Gen. 15:16 and Mt. 23:32-33.
[31]See Heb. 7:27; 9:12; 10:10.

The result of filling up the measure is the wrath (the wrath to come) which means here damnation (or lack of salvation) as is clear from 5:9: "For God has not destined us for wrath, but to obtain salvation through our Lord Jesus Christ."[32] Thus the Apostle meant here that the opposition of the Jews to the spreading of God's word as offered by the prophets, Jesus Christ, and the apostles, puts them under the sword of damnation (*i.e.*, lack of salvation) "εἰς τέλος—until the end," *i.e.*, until the second coming of the Lord Jesus Christ. The way to prevent that sword from falling and executing damnation is the acceptance of Jesus Christ by endorsing the apostolic teaching.

v.17. Ἡμεῖς δέ, ἀδελφοί, ἀπορφανισθέντες ἀφ᾽ ὑμῶν πρὸς καιρὸν ὥρας προσώπῳ οὐ καρδίᾳ, περισσοτέρως ἐσπουδάσαμεν τὸ πρόσωπον ὑμῶν ἰδεῖν ἐν πολλῇ ἐπιθυμίᾳ.

But since we were bereft of you, brethren, for a short time, in face/presence not in heart, we endeavored the more eagerly and with great desire to see your face;

After having finished reminding the Thessalonians of all that has happened between him and them since his arrival and during his stay in Thessalonica, Paul moves to the second part of his apologia, where he stresses the fact that his pure love and extreme care for them did not cease or become

---

[32]See also Rom. 2:5, 8, 21; 9:22, Phil. 1:28; 3:18-19.

lukewarm after his fleeing from there. And this is precisely
the topic of the following passage in our epistle (2:17-3:13).

Paul starts off with using a verb found only here in the
entire New Testament: 'But since we were *bereft of you*,
brethren, for a short time . . ." The use of the verb "ἀπορφα-
νίζω—to be orphan/to be bereft of" to indicate his missing,
and longing for, the Thessalonians is a clear proof that his
mind was still overwhelmed with the idea of his fatherhood
(or motherhood!) toward them which he expressed in a
unique way in verses 7-9 and 11 above. Now the state of
orphanhood/bereavement between two beloved is very difficult at its beginning; hence the Apostle's feeling of the
acuteness of the separation which happened "for a short
time."

The actual expression is "πρὸς καιρὸν ὥρας." The noun
καιρός means instant, moment, given time, specific or defined
moment; whereas the noun ὥρα means hour or short time, and takes
sometimes—as in English—the meaning of a given instant. The
former word appears in I Cor. 7:5, and the latter in II Cor. 7:8
and Gal. 2:5, with the meaning of a short period of time. In all
these cases the term is preceded by the preposition "πρός—to/
toward/for." Thus in I Corinthians we read πρὸς καιρόν, while
in II Corinthians and Galatians πρὸς ὥραν. From there it appears
that the use of both terms together after πρός in our text indicates
that the intended is a short period of time.

Paul insists immediately that the separation was an absence
of faces, not a cleavage of hearts. But this in turn was
precisely the reason that made his longing for the Thessalonians a great one (ἐν πολλῇ ἐπιθυμίᾳ) and multiplied
(περισσοτέρως) his desire (ἐσπουδάσαμεν, aorist of
σπουδάζω—to make an effort, to desire) to see their faces
(compare 3:10).

v.18. διότι ἠθελήσαμεν ἐλθεῖν πρὸς ὑ-
μᾶς, ἐγὼ μὲν Παῦλος καὶ ἅπαξ
καὶ δίς, καὶ ἐνέκοψεν ἡμᾶς ὁ Σατανᾶς.

therefore we wanted to come to you—myself,
Paul, many a time—but Satan hindered us.

The bereavement of the Thessalonians' faces produced a
powerful longing, whose result was positive in that the
Apostle tried his best to see them again, and this his effort
in turn was transformed in a will (ἠθελήσαμεν) to come
(ἐλθεῖν) to them. Here, the Apostle writes in brackets, as
it were, "myself, Paul" to underline that he wanted *personally* (ἐγώ) to travel and that his decision to send Timothy
(3:2) was but a second choice. To be sure, he tried to come
personally to them many a time, again and again (καὶ ἅπαξ
καὶ δίς).

> Καὶ ἅπαξ καὶ δίς does not mean "once and twice" in the narrow
> sense, or else Paul would have simply said δίς or καὶ δίς, *i.e.*, twice. This
> is confirmed by what we read in Phil. 4:16: "for even in Thessalonica you
> sent me help once and again—καὶ ἅπαξ καὶ δίς." Here again what is
> intended is that the faithful of Philippi took care of the Apostle's needs
> every time the necessity arose.

However, it was "the devil—ὁ Σατανᾶς"[33] himself who
brought to naught all these efforts. And the reason is that
the devil knows but too well that the gospel brings salvation
to all men and consequently defeat to him and to his kingdom
of darkness.

---

[33]See our study of the word "the devil—ὁ Σατανᾶς" in Appendix IV.

v.19. τὶς γὰρ ἡμῶν ἡ ἐλπὶς ἢ χαρὰ ἢ
ἢ στέφανος καυχήσεως—ἢ οὐχὶ
καὶ ὑμεῖς—ἔμπροσθεν τοῦ κυρίου
ἡμῶν Ἰησοῦ ἐν τῇ αὐτοῦ παρουσίᾳ;

For what is our hope or joy or crown of
boasting/pride— what indeed but you—before our Lord Jesus at his coming?

At the mention of the devil and his continual effort to
hinder the apostolic mission, Paul's mind is suddenly overwhelmed with the image of the Lord Jesus as judge of all at
His second coming.[34] And Paul is fully aware that the issue
at stake in his case will be essentially whether he will have
accomplished his work as apostle or not: "... For I would
rather die than have any one deprive me of my ground for
boasting. For necessity is laid upon me. *Woe to me if I do
not preach the gospel!*" (I Cor. 9:15-16). In this same sense
the Apostle is saying that his hope, joy, and crown of pride
are the Thessalonians themselves, *i.e.*, those who have accepted the faith at his hands. Why? Because they will be
an indubitable proof before the Judge that Paul has done
his duty, and thus his Master will say to him: "Well done,
good and faithful servant; you have been faithful over a
little, I will set you over much; enter into the joy of your
master" (Mt. 25:21 and 23).

Moreover we do know from the rest of the Pauline writings that each of the three terms used here (joy, crown,
pride/boasting) is intimately related, in Paul's mind, to his

---

[34]See our study of the word "παρουσία—presence/coming" in Appendix
V.

missionary activity and to his awareness that he will be
judged on the basis of his performing this duty, indeed on
whether he will have been successful in it or not.[35] How much
more, then, is this the case when all of these three terms
together run under his pen! This is also an indication of his
great worry for the Thessalonians' faith.

v.20. ὑμεῖς γάρ ἐστε ἡ δόξα ἡμῶν καὶ ἡ χαρά.

For you are our glory and joy.

In this verse Paul emphasizes the idea mentioned in the
previous one. Thus after the rhetorical question comes the
positive statement: *You* are our glory and joy.

---

[35]For the word "χαρά—joy" see I Thess. 3:7-9; Rom. 15:31-32; 16:19;
II Cor. 1:24; 7:9; 13:9; Phil. 1:4-5, 18; 2:2, 17-18; 3:17-4:1; Col. 1:24;
2:5; Philem. 7. As for the word "στέφανος—crown" see I Cor. 9:23-27;
Phil. 3:17-4:1; II Tim. 4:6-8. Finally for the word "καύχησις—pride/
boasting" see Rom. 15:17-19; I Cor. 9:15-16; 15:29-32; II Cor. 1:12-14;
11:7-11; Gal. 6:13-14; Phil. 2:16-17; II Thess. 1:3-5.

CHAPTER THREE

v.1. Διὸ μηκέτι στέγοντες ηὐδοκήσα-
μεν καταλειφθῆναι ἐν ᾿Αθήναις
μόνοι.

Therefore when we could bear it no longer,
we were willing to be left behind alone in
Athens.

After the parenthesis of verses 2:19-20, the Apostle resumes
his main thought by saying that he could bear no longer his
not being able to see the Thessalonians, although the hindering reasons were overwhelming (2:18). This shows in a
unique way his extreme love for "the beloved brethren" in
Thessalonica. Indeed the verb στέγω has the meaning of
suffering under an extreme difficulty (see I Cor. 9:21 and
13:7), and appears twice in our passage: here and in v.5.

Due to this unwillingness to suffer separation, Paul was
willing to be left alone in Athens. The use of the verb
"καταλείπομαι—to be left behind" instead of "παραμέ-
νω—to remain" sheds a light on the Apostle's situation in
Athens. After his bitter experience in that city (Acts
17:16-34), he needed the comfort of his preferred disciple
(see Introduction); yet necessity obliged him to take a decision
whose result was that Timothy left him "alone—μόνοι" in
Athens.

Although μόνοι is in the plural, it refers only to the person of Paul (and not to that of Silvanus also). Indeed here the speaker and the doer are but one: v.5 is but a condensed repetition of vv.1-3a after the parenthesis in vv.3b-4. Let us heed the parallelism between them, of meaning as well as of vocabulary:

διὸ (1) μηκέτι (2) στέγοντες (3) . . . ἐπέμψαμεν (4) . . . εἰς τό (5) . . . τῆς πίστεως ὑμῶν (6)
(v.1-2)

διὰ τοῦτο (1) κἀγὼ μηκέτι (2) στέγων (3) ἔπεμψα
(4) εἰς τό (5) . . . τὴν πίστιν ὑμῶν (6) (v.5)

In both these texts the idea is that due to his not being able to bear it any longer, Paul (notice the first person singular in v.5) sent Timothy to check on the Thessalonians' faith, for fear that somehow the tempter would have made some of them fall in the snare of being disturbed by their afflictions.

Hence Paul consented to forget all his personal cares for the sake of his first duty, namely preach the gospel as well as make sure that it is firmly implanted in the hearts of those newly come to the faith.

vv.2-3a. καὶ ἐπέμψαμεν Τιμόθεον, τὸν ἀ-
δελφὸν ἡμῶν καὶ συνεργὸν τοῦ
Θεοῦ ἐν τῷ εὐαγγελίῳ τοῦ Χριστοῦ, εἰς τὸ στηρίξαι ὑμᾶς καὶ πα-
ρακαλέσαι ὑπὲρ τῆς πίστεως ὑμῶν
τὸ μηδένα σαίνεσθαι ἐν ταῖς θλίψε-
σιν ταύταις.

and we sent Timothy, our brother and God's fellow-worker in the gospel of Christ, to es-tablish and exhort you in (the matter of)

your faith, so that no one be swayed by these
afflictions.

Our preference for he reading καὶ συνεργὸν τοῦ Θεοῦ ἐν τῷ εὐαγγελίῳ τοῦ Χριστοῦ over the others found in the various manuscripts
goes back to two reasons: first, it is definitely the one most difficult to
account for (*lectio difficilior*) and, secondly, all the other readings can be
explained by it.

It is impressive that we find in the manuscripts no less than eight different renderings. This fact indicates that the copyists were faced with a
great difficulty and that they tried to overcome it by suggesting corrections
which—they thought—would reflect better Paul's intent. Here are the most
important:

1) and the fellow-worker, resp. our[1]co-worker—καὶ συνεργόν
2) and the servant—καὶ διάκονον
3) and the servant of God—καὶ διάκονον τοῦ Θεοῦ
4) the servant and co-worker of God—διάκονον καὶ συνεργὸν τοῦ
   Θεοῦ
5) the servant of God and our co-worker—καὶ διάκονον τοῦ Θεοῦ
   καὶ συνεργὸν ἡμῶν

It is clear that all these alternatives are endeavors to tone down Paul's
boldness in his saying that his disciple Timothy is God's co-worker whenever he is preaching Christ's good tidings (see also I Cor. 3:9).

Paul qualifies Timothy here as συνεργὸν τοῦ Θεοῦ,
i.e., God's partner in the same work or the co-worker of God.
The Apostle uses this same expression when speaking of
himself and Apollos (I Cor. 3:9) and thus of any apostle.
What might be its meaning?

A careful reading of the passage I Cor. 3:5-9 will show
that the intent is not that God plants, waters and makes
grow in one place, while the apostle does a similar work
in another, but rather that both are dealing with *the same
plant*. Thus the meaning is not that the apostle produces his
own plantation or building or temple parallel to God's work,
but that the plantation is one, so is the building and so is
the temple (3:16), namely God's. Consequently the intent is

---

[1]We added here in the translation the possessive adjective "our" since
in this reading the noun "co-worker" is in conjunction with the preceding
"*our* brother— τὸν ἀδελφὸν ἡμῶν."

that the apostle is a servant upon whom God has bestowed the gift/grace of performing *some of His* (i.e. *God's*) *work* (3:5-7). Now the work intended in both passages (I Thess. 3:2 and I Cor. 3:5-9) is the preaching activity, and we have seen earlier (see the comment on 1:5) that the gospel is God's and Christ's first, and that is does not become the apostle's except insofar as he bears it, *i.e.*, inasmuch as he becomes its person.

That each of us be "co-worker of God—συνεργὸν τοῦ Θεοῦ" means that God's gospel becomes ours, God's work ours, God's intent ours, in other words that we integrate God's dream . . . or better, that we be integrated into God's dream! And His dream is nothing less than the kingdom of heaven!

As to the purpose of sending Timothy, it is to confirm and exhort. The verb "στηρίζω—to make firm/to establish/ to confirm" appears only six times in the Pauline epistles, four of which in the two letters to the Thessalonians (I Thess. 3:2, 13; II Thess. 2:17; 3:3); which reflects how much the Apostle was worried about the faithful in that city. Now this act of making firm, confirming, Timothy will do through his exhortation in all that pertains to their faith. The beauty of the verb παρακαλέω lies in that it means both to exhort and to comfort at the same time. Thus Timothy's exhortation to the Thessalonians must have as a result true consolation, which is reflected in that the ultimate aim of such an exhortation is that none of the believers be moved/swayed by the afflictions they were undergoing.

The use of the demonstrative "these—ταύταις" along with afflictions shows that the affliction lived by the Thessalonians at their acceptance of the gospel (see 1:6) was still upon them at the time of writing. On the other hand, the plural use of "afflictions—θλίψεις" (compare 1:6 and 3:7) might be another indication that the situation was so dangerous as to sway the Thessalonians away from their faith.

v.3b-4. αὐτοὶ γὰρ οἴδατε ὅτι εἰς τοῦτο
κείμεθα· καὶ γὰρ ὅτε πρὸς ὑμᾶς
ἦμεν, προελέγομεν ὑμῖν ὅτι μέλλο-
μεν θλίβεσθαι, καθὼς καὶ ἐγένετο
καὶ οἴδατε.

You yourselves know that this is to be our
lot. For when we were with you, we told you
beforehand that we were to suffer affliction;
just as it has come to pass, and as you know.

Paul finishes by affirming once more that difficulties and
afflictions are an integral part of the subject matter of the
gospel:[2] "You yourselves know that this is to be our lot—
εἰς τοῦτο κείμεθα." Then he adds, in order to exhort and
confirm them, that he did inform them beforehand while he
was among them that such afflictions were bound to take
place and thus that there was no reason to be shaken.

v.5. διὰ τοῦτο κἀγὼ μηκέτι στέγων ἔ-
πεμψα εἰς τὸ γνῶναι τὴν πίστιν
ὑμῶν, μή πως ἐπείρασεν ὑμᾶς ὁ
πειράζων καὶ εἰς κενὸν γένηται ὁ
κόπος ἡμῶν.

For this reason, when I could bear it no longer,
I sent that I might know your faith, for fear

[2]See 1:6.

that somehow the tempter had tempted you
and that our labor would be in vain.

Here Paul repeats that he sent "in order to know—εἰς
τὸ γνῶναι" their faith, *i.e.*, that he might check on the
condition of their faith. Yet this verse brings up two new
aspects of his fear that the Thessalonians might have been
shaken in their faith.

The first one has to do with the cause for such an attitude, or better, with its author, namely the tempter. The
Apostle makes it clear that difficulties, temptations and afflictions in the believer's life are all intended and the direct
result of the work of the devil, whose sole occupation is
to hinder the gospel's effectiveness. Thus the devil himself
has put the Thessalonians under the predicament of tempta-
tion in order to shake their faith as well as to hold back
Paul from coming to their rescue (2:18).

The other aspect of the Apostle's fear is linked to the
result of such shaking of the faith, namely bringing to naught
all of his efforts to spread Christ's gospel.[3]

v.6. ῎Αρτι δὲ ἐλθόντος Τιμοθέου πρὸς
ἡμᾶς ἀφ᾽ ὑμῶν καὶ εὐαγγελισαμένου ἡμῖν τὴν πίστιν καὶ τὴν ἀγά-
πην ὑμῶν, καὶ ὅτι ἔχετε μνείαν
ἡμῶν ἀγαθὴν πάντοτε, ἐπιποθοῦν-
τες ἡμᾶς ἰδεῖν καθάπερ καὶ ἡμεῖς
ὑμᾶς,

---

[3]Regarding the word "κόπος—labor" see 1:3; as for the expression "εἰς
κενόν—in vain" see 2:1.

But now that Timothy has come to us from
you, and has brought us the good news of your
faith and love and reported that you always
remember us kindly and long to see us, as
we long to see you—

After having described that difficult and tiring stage of
his fear (2:17-3:15) Paul moves to expressing his feelings
after Timothy's return to him from Thessalonica (3:6-13).
It is quite impressive that this canvas is totally different
from the previous one. Here Paul is overwhelmed with
thoughts of comfort (v.7), breathing of life (v.8), thanksgiving and joy (v.9), which culminate in a prayer to God
the Father and the Lord Jesus (vv.11-13).

Paul's great cheerfulness at the news brought to him by
Timothy is reflected in the terms themselves. Thus Timothy
did not simply inform the Apostle of the Thessalonians'
faith and love, but he "evangelized/brought the good news
to—εὐαγγελισαμένου" him of such. In all the Pauline
writings—indeed in the whole New Testament[4]—the verb
"εὐαγγελίζομαι—to bring good tidings" always has the
meaning of bringing the good news of the gospel, *i.e.*, the
news of the kingdom and of salvation. The exception in
this our verse is a clear indication that the news of the
Thessalonians' firmness in their stand for the gospel he has
brought them had the same effect on him as the gospel
itself. The news that the gospel has borne fruits is gladdening, and the steadfastness of such fruits is itself *a gospel!*
None could feel such a reality except a true apostle who
knows well that the lack of steadfastness in bearing fruit
means that his efforts were in vain, and that consequently

---

[4]Except Lk. 1:19.

he will have no ground for joy or crown of boasting or glory at the coming of the just Judge (2:19-20; 3:9).

Now, in Paul's eyes the important practical outcome is that the Thessalonian faithful show a mutuality of feeling toward him: as he always prays for them, they also do the same for him,[5] and as he misses them, they also long to meet him again. That he cares for his children and they for him is a soothing balm on the Apostle's wounds.

v.7. διὰ τοῦτο παρεκλήθημεν, ἀδελφοί, ἐφ᾽ ὑμῖν ἐπὶ πάσῃ τῇ ἀνάγκῃ καὶ θλίψει ἡμῶν διὰ τῆς ὑμῶν πίστεως,

for this reason, brethren, in all our distress and affliction we have been comforted about you through your faith;

The Apostle here opens wide his heart and confesses that the result of his care to strengthen and comfort the Thessalonians has fully reverted to him in an expression of comfort for himself (see also II Cor. 1:3-7); as for the source of this consolation, it is the good news regarding their faith (see also Rom. 1:12).

v.8. ὅτι νῦν ζῶμεν ἐὰν ὑμεῖς στήκετε ἐν κυρίῳ.

---

[5]We have shown in our comments on 1:3 that the expression "μνείαν ἀγαθήν—good/kind remembrance" meant prayer.

for now we live (breathe life), if you stand
fast in the Lord.

In this verse Paul's comment on the news brought back
by Timothy attains its climax. The meaning of his saying is
the following: Now we have breathed again and life has
come back to us, when we heard the good news from
Timothy; however, you ought to know that this breath of
life will remain if you stand fast in the Lord, *i.e.*, if the status
of your faith is fully reflected in our being itself.

vv.9-10. τίνα γὰρ εὐχαριστίαν δυνάμεθα
τῷ Θεῷ ἀνταποδοῦναι περὶ ὑμῶν
ἐπὶ πάσῃ τῇ χαρᾷ ᾗ χαίρομεν
δι᾽ ὑμᾶς ἔμπροσθεν τοῦ Θεοῦ ἡμῶν,
νυκτὸς καὶ ἡμέρας ὑπερεκπερισσοῦ δεόμενοι εἰς τὸ ἰδεῖν ὑμῶν τὸ
πρόσωπον καὶ καταρτίσαι τὰ ὑστε-
ρήματα τῆς πίστεως ὑμῶν;

For what thanksgiving can we render to God
for you, for all the joy we feel for your sake
before God, praying earnestly night and day
that we may see you face to face and supply
what is lacking in your faith?

The Apostle moves on to giving thanks to God for the
comfort resulting from the gladdening news. It is to be noted

that the expression of this thanks in the form of a question is an indication that Paul's tongue stumbled totally before God's gift surpassing every imagination, namely the true and eschatological joy before the dread judgment seat of God (see 2:19-20). But the steadfastness of the Thessalonians throughout the harsh afflictions that befell them until now is a clear indication that they will carry on their struggle until the second coming of the Lord (see 3:13). Therefore the Apostle starts to feel already now—though only in part— the infinite joy the Lord will bestow upon him on the last day. Paul is thus right when he asks himself whether he is able to find sufficient and suitable words of thanks to offer for the joy that cannot be repaid.

The "joy—χαρά" intended here is not only a deep human joy, but also and rather the full and eschatological joy—the joy of the heavenly kingdom—which God will bestow upon His saints at the day of the parousia. Indeed:

1) We read in our verse "all the joy—πάση τῆ χαρᾷ" with the definite article and not "all joy—πάση χαρᾷ." Thus the Apostle does not seem to have in mind a piling up of different joys resulting from different occasions.

2) Paul's saying that this joy is "for your sake/because of you— δι' ὑμᾶς" reminds us of the verses 2:19-20. Now, the word "joy— χαρά" is the only one mentioned twice among the terms used in relation to the Apostle's situation at the second coming of the Lord and on both occasions the reason and basis for that joy are the Thessalonians themselves.

3) It is clear that the idea in both instances (2:19-20 and 3:9) is the Thessalonians' steadfastness in faith and the Apostle's fear of their possible shakiness.

4) The expression "before our God—ἔμπροσθεν τοῦ Θεοῦ" appears again in v.13. Now vv.11-13 contain the prayer resulting from the question put in our v.9. Indeed, there the Apostle asks that the opportunity be given to him to visit Thessalonica (v.11) and that God establish the hearts of the faithful there unblamable in holiness at the coming of the Lord Jesus (v.13).

Verse 10 confirms what we found in 1:2, namely that

thanksgiving is an integral part of Paul's daily prayer. Now, due to the circumstances, this prayer was transformed into an earnest petition, night and day, that God would allow the Apostle to see the Thessalonians again in order to supplement what is lacking in their faith.

Two important notes: (a) Paul's prime concern regarding the Thessalonians is the health of their faith, not of their bodies (see 1:3). (b) Faith is not a solidified entity, but a reality that grows or shrinks, becomes stronger or weaker, and it is the Apostle's duty to keep track of the faith of those he has evangelized, as the good shepherd does not lose sight of his sheep.

v.11. Αὐτὸς δὲ ὁ Θεὸς καὶ πατὴρ ἡμῶν καὶ ὁ κύριος ἡμῶν Ἰησοῦς κατευθύναι τὴν ὁδὸν ἡμῶν πρὸς ἡμᾶς.

Now may our God and Father Himself and our Lord Jesus direct our way to you;

Paul ends here in vv.11-13 by addressing a prayer to God whereby it clearly appears that his ultimate concern is that the Thessalonians remain anchored in their faith and love and holiness until the day of the Lord. Thus he asks that God the Father and the Lord Jesus direct his way to Thessalonica, knowing well that, God willing, he will succeed one day to make this trip in spite of the opposing endeavors of the devil (2:18).

It is striking that in the original Greek text the verb "κατευθύνω—to direct/to set forth" (here in the aorist optative) is used here in the singular although the plural

would be expected since there is more than one subject. This
is a clear proof that, in Paul's mind, God the Father and
the Lord Jesus are the one source of the same action, though
the one is not the other. The prayer is addressed to both and
each receive it, yet the action is one since God is one. Here
is thus another example that confirms what we have found
in 1:1, namely that the Father and the Son are two persons
with one effect, action or energy.

v.12. ὑμᾶς δὲ ὁ κύριος πλεονάσαι καὶ
περισσεύσαι τῇ ἀγάπῃ εἰς ἀλλήλους καὶ εἰς πάντας, καθάπερ καὶ
ἡμεῖς εἰς ὑμᾶς.

and may the Lord make you increase and
abound in love to one another and to all
men, as we do to you,

After praying that he may come to Thessalonica in order
to confirm the Christians in their faith (see v.10) Paul turns
to the other aspect of faith, namely love (see the comments
on 1:3). The Apostle knows well that the Thessalonians
are an example of love (see 1:3); yet he also knows that
love sums up the whole law (see Rom. 13:8-10 and Gal.
5:13-14). Therefore he prays that the Lord may fill them
completely — πλεονάσαι—, even that He may make them
overflow — περισσεύσαι — with that love that pulls them to
each other and all of them into one family.

Paul ends by giving himself as a living example of the
kind of love he is talking about, so that his words might
not sound purely theoretical. The Thessalonians must have

understood his intention since they had experienced his love
for them (see 2:7-12, 17-18; 3:1-5).

v.13. εἰς τὸ στηρίξαι ὑμῶν τὰς καρδίας
ἀμέμπτους ἐν ἁγιωσύνῃ ἔμπροσθεν τοῦ Θεοῦ καὶ πατρὸς ἡμῶν
ἐν τῇ παρουσίᾳ τοῦ κυρίου ἡμῶν
Ἰησοῦ μετὰ πάντων τῶν ἁγίων
αὐτοῦ. [Ἀμὴν]

so that he may establish your hearts unblamable in holiness before our God and
Father, at the coming of our Lord Jesus with
all his saints. [Amen]

Paul's concern is that the heart, even the whole being (see
the comments on 2:4), of the faithful be in a full state of
holiness before God the Judge at the coming of the Lord
Jesus. Now this the Apostle's stand can be explained by the
fact that the concept of holiness—ἁγιωσύνη—in the New
Testament summarizes all that which Christians should be.
Thus, in the early church, the believers were also called "the
saints—οἱ ἅγιοι" (Col. 1:22).[6] The reason for that is obvious
from what Peter writes: "... but as he who called you is
holy, be holy yourselves in all your conduct; since it is written:
You shall be holy, for I am holy" (I Pet. 1:15-16).

One might ask: who are the saints that will accompany
our Lord Jesus at His second coming? They are first of all

[6]See especially Acts (9:13, 32, 41), Paul's epistles (Rom. 1:7; I Cor.
1:2; II Cor. 1:1; Eph. 1:1; Col. 1:2; Philem. 5 and 7) and Revelation.

the angels, God's servants, as appears from the New Testament.[7] However, the saints here might as well be all the righteous that fell asleep in the Lord and will come in His party at His coming in glory. Indeed Paul writes elsewhere: "Do you not know that the saints will judge the world? And if the world is to be judged by you, are you incompetent to try trivial cases? Do you not know that we are to judge angels? How much more, matters pertaining to this life!" (I Cor. 6:2-3). The saints here are clearly the believers (v.2) who will even judge the angels (v.3).

The word "ἀμήν—Amen" is included at the end of this verse in quite a number of important manuscripts: "Codex Sinaiticus," A, D and the old Italic. It is difficult to decide whether this word was added in these manuscripts or deleted from the others. It is possible that Paul has thus concluded his prayer; it is possible as well that ἀμήν was introduced here after the use of this text as a liturgical reading in the early church.

---

[7]Mt. 13:39, 41, 49; 16:27; 24-31; 25:31; Mk. 13:24; Lk. 12:8-9; II Thess. 1:7; Rev. 3:5; 5:11; 7:11.

CHAPTER FOUR

v.1. Λοιπὸν οὖν, ἀδελφοί, ἐρωτῶμεν ὑ-
μᾶς καὶ παρακαλοῦμεν ἐν κυρίῳ
Ἰησοῦ, ἵνα καθὼς παρελάβετε
παρ' ἡμῶν τὸ πῶς δεῖ ὑμᾶς περιπατεῖν καὶ ἀρέσκειν Θεῷ, καθὼς
καὶ περιπατεῖτε, ἵνα περισσεύητε
μᾶλλον.

Finally, brethren, we demand from you and
exhort you in the Lord Jesus, that as you
learned from us how you ought to live and
to please God, just as you are doing, you do
so more and more.

The verb ἐρωτῶ usually means "to inquire" and thus "to request," "to ask." Yet we prefer to translate it here as "to demand" which has the connotation of order. The reason is that Paul usually uses the verb "πα-ρακαλῶ—to exhort, to entreat," to request something specific from the faithful, whereas ἐρωτῶ appears only four times in his writings (Phil. 4:3; I Thess. 4:1; 5:12; II Thess. 2:1) and in all these instances the intent is an order:

1) In Phil. 4:2-3 the Apostle exhorts/entreats Evodia and Syntyche to be in agreement, whereas he demands that his true fellow worker help them.

2) In I Thess. 5:12 Paul orders the Thessalonians to obey those who are over them, whereas he exhorts them (5:14) to accomplish their other duties.

3) In II Thess. 2:1-2 the Apostle's clear intent is to forbid the Thessalonians from accepting any other teaching besides that which he has delivered to them (see also v.5).

133

4) It is true that both verbs are linked in our text; however, the meaning is clear since Paul continues in v.2: "For you know what instructions—παραγγελίας—we gave you through the Lord Jesus." The word παραγγελία has the meaning of instruction or commandment, and thus reflects an order. Besides, we find in II Thess. 3:12 the verbs παρακαλῶ and "παραγγέλλω—to command/to order" linked in the same way as in our verse: "Now such persons we command and exhort in the Lord Jesus Christ to do their work in quietness and to earn their own living."

Starting with chapter four the Apostle moves to a different topic; as is shown by the use of "λοιπόν—besides/after that/furthermore" at the beginning of our verse.[1] Thus, after having finished defending the correctness of his teaching, his good behavior and his extreme love for the Thessalonians—in a word: the truthfulness of his apostleship[2]—in the first three chapters, Paul proceeds to underline some major practical points and clarify some instructional matters, on the basis of what Timothy has informed him regarding the situation in the church of Thessalonica upon his return from there.

The first point picked up by the Apostle is fornication. Thus he starts by reminding them that he has previously taught them what their behavior[3] ought to be in order to be well-pleasing to God, and he makes it clear that he is aware that they are doing their best to follow that path. Yet he exhorts them in the Lord Jesus, he even demands from them, to make an extra effort in this direction. This indicates that the situation was not actually as it should be. This is anyhow reflected in the length of the passage (seven verses) which Paul devotes to this issue.

---

[1] Compare the use of λοιπόν in II Cor. 13:11; Phil. 3:1; 4:8; II Thess. 3:1.

[2] See our comments on 1:2.

[3] See our comments on the verb "περιπατέω—to behave" in 2:12.

v.2. οἴδατε γὰρ τίνας παραγγελίας ἐ-
δώκαμεν ὑμῖν διὰ τοῦ κυρίου Ἰησοῦ.

For you know what instructions we gave you
through (from) the Lord Jesus.

This verse underlines that the Apostle's request in v.1
has the tonality of an order, since he reminds the Thessalonians of the instructions he has left them with. The noun
"παραγγελία—instruction" appears only here at Paul's
hand,[4] whereas the verb "παραγγέλλω—to command/to
leave instructions" is found only seven times,[4] five of which
in the letters to the Thessalonians. Besides, we do read here
that the Apostle gave those instructions "διά—from, through"
the Lord Jesus. This brings the meaning of this text close to
that in I Cor. 7:10-11 where Paul writes: "To the married
I give charge, not I but the Lord, that the wife should not
separate from her husband . . . and that the husband should
not divorce his wife," differentiating between the Lord's
commandment and his own saying, as he continues in v.12:
"To the rest I say, not the Lord . . ." The conclusion then
is that the Apostle's teaching regarding fornication has its
source in the commandment of Jesus Himself.

v.3. τοῦτο γάρ ἐστιν θέλημα τοῦ Θεοῦ,
ἁγιασμὸς ὑμῶν, ἀπέχεσθαι ὑμᾶς
ἀπὸ τῆς πορνείας,

---

[4]We except the pastoral epistle I Tim.
[5]Isaiah 29:16; 45:9-11.

For this is the will of God, your sanctification: that you abstain from fornication;

That which was said about holiness in 3:13 is rendered
clearly in this verse. Here the Apostle states already in his
first letter what he will come back to time and again as
well as in detail in his later writings, namely: God's will
for the believers is summed up in their "sanctification—
ἁγιασμός," in their becoming saints. Could it have been
otherwise when we know from the Holy Scriptures that God's
essential attribute is that He is holy, that He alone is holy?
Therefore He calls the faithful to be sanctified, *i.e.*, to become like Him, to become divine, to be such as the people
would see God's light reflected in their faces. Thus "Thy
will be done on earth as it is in heaven" is a prayer that
God's presence may fill the whole earth through our holiness, us the Christians.

After this short statement on the direct relation of holiness to God's will, the Apostle proceeds to the field of
practical application concentrating on a specific topic: "Your
sanctification means that you abstain from fornication." The
stress on fornication as well as its mention first in the list
of sins (I Cor. 6:9; Gal. 5:19; Eph. 5:3, 5; Col. 3:5) is a
clear indication that this habit was quite widespread in those
days; this is confirmed by the data we have about the first-
century Roman Empire. Regarding the grievousness of the
sin of fornication from the Christian perspective, see I Cor.
6:9-20, especially verses 11, 15, 19, 20.

vv.4-5. εἰδέναι ἕκαστον ὑμῶν τὸ ἑαυτοῦ
σκεῦος στᾶσθαι ἐν ἁγιασμῷ καὶ

τιμῇ, μὴ ἐν πάθει ἐπιθυμίας καθάπερ καὶ τὰ ἔθνη τὰ μὴ εἰδότα τὸν
Θεόν,

that each one of you know how to control
his body in holiness and honor, not in the
passion of lust like heathen who do not know
God

Interpreters are at odds concerning the meaning of "σκεῦος—vessel" in
v.4. Some understand it as "the body," while others think that the intended
here is "the wife." Which would be correct?

The following are the reasons that make us opt for the first alternative:

1) Paul uses σκεῦος to indicate the human being himself. Thus in
Rom. 9:20-24 we read: "But who are you, *a man*, to answer back to God?
Will what is molded say to its molder, "Why have you made me thus?[5]
Has the potter no right over the clay,[6] to make out of the same lump one
vessel for beauty and another for menial use? What if God, desiring to
show his wrath and to make known his power, has endured with much
patience the *vessels of wrath* made for destruction, in order to make known
the riches of his glory for the *vessels of mercy* which *he has prepared
beforehand for glory,*[7] even *us* whom he has called,[7] not from the Jews only
but also from the Gentiles?" Elsewhere the Apostle writes: "But *we have
this treasure in earthen vessels,* to show that the transcendent power belongs
to God and not to *us*" (II Cor. 4:7). Finally in II Tim. 2:20-21 we find:
"...*If anyone purifies himself* . . . then he will be *a vessel for noble use,*
consecrated and useful to the master of the house, ready for any good
work."

2) Those who advocate that σκεῦος in I Thess. 4:4 means "the wife"
refer to the following text of I Pet.: "Likewise you husbands, live con-
siderately with them, bestowing honor on the woman/wife as the weaker
vessel—σκεύει" (3:7). The objection to such an interpretation stems from
the fact that the original text read: "ἀσθενεστέρῳ σκεύει τῷ γυναικείῳ," whose literal translation is as follows: "as a weaker vessel, that is
the womanly one." This translation takes into consideration the fact that
"γυναικείῳ—womanly" is an adjective modifying "σκεύει—vessel" and
that the definite article τῷ does not refer to "weaker vessel," but to
"womanly." Thus the expression "τῷ γυναικείῳ—the womanly one"
qualifies (is an adjective to) the preceding and does not define it. The
meaning of the verse is then: "bestowing honor on a weaker body/being/
person, I mean the womanly one."

[6]Jer. 18:6.
[7]Rom. 8:30.

3) To say that every faithful should keep/acquire "his own vessel" in holiness and honor—ἐν ἁγιασμῷ καὶ τιμῇ—and not in the passion of lust—μὴ ἐν πάθει ἐπιθυμίας—indicates that the latter idea is in opposition to the former. A thorough study of the use of the two words "πάθος—passion"—and "ἐπιθυμία—lust/desire" in the Pauline writings will soon convince us that the intended is always the fleshly passion in fornication,[8] whereas the Apostle never speaks of passion and lust in the context of married life.

4) The concept of "sanctification/holiness—ἁγιασμός" in our verse is directly linked to the abiding of the Holy Spirit in the faithful: "For God has not called us for uncleanness, but in holiness. Therefore whoever disregards this, disregards not man but God, who gives his Holy Spirit to you" (vv.7-8). As to the result of the Holy Spirit's abiding in us, it is, the sanctification of our bodies, as appears from the following texts: Rom. 8:9, 11; I Cor. 3:16-18; 6:18-20.

In these two verses the Apostle explains the meaning of abstention from fornication. He emphasizes that God's will regarding our body is that it be kept in holiness and honor. The mention of honor along with holiness is a clear indication that what is meant is not human honor, but that which God bestows and which so often appears in parallel with God's glory to which He calls us.[9] The relation of this honor to the purity of the body from all fornication is made clear in Rom. 1:24-26a where Paul writes: "Therefore God gave them up in the lusts of their hearts to impurity, to the dishonoring of their bodies among themselves, because they exchanged the truth about God for a lie and worshipped and served the creature rather than the creator, who is blessed for ever! Amen. For this reason God gave them up to dishonorable passions."[10]

To keep our body in holiness and honor means to keep it from the passion of lust. The term "πάθος—passion" appears always with "ἐπιθυμία—lust/desire" (Rom. 1:24-26; Col. 3:5; I Thess. 4:5),[11] and both along with "πορνεία—

---

[8]See Rom. 1:24.

[9]Rom. 2:7, 10; I Tim. 1:17; Heb. 2:7, 9; I Pet. 1:7; II Pet. 1:17; Rev. 4:9, 11; 5:12-13; 7:12.

[10]Note the use of the exact same words in I Thess. 4:3-7 and Rom. 1:24-26.

[11]See also Rom. 7:5-7 and Gal. 5:24 where we find the word πάθημα with ἐπιθυμία.

fornication" in the Epistle to the Colossians: "Put to death therefore what is earthly in you: *fornication*, impurity, *passion*, *evil desire*, and covetousness, which is idolatry" (3:5), as well as in the letter to the Galatians: "Now the works of the flesh are plain: *fornication*, impurity, licenteousness . . . And those who belong to Christ Jesus have crucified the flesh with its *passions* and *desire*" (5:19, 24).

Finally the Apostle says that the works of passion are done by those who do not know God, and are unworthy of the faithful who have turned to the worship of the living and true God (1:9). In other words, the fornicator behaves as if he were still away from God.

v.6. τὸ μὴ ὑπερβαίνειν καὶ πλεονεκτεῖν ἐν τῷ πράγματι τὸν ἀδελφὸν αὐτοῦ, διότι ἔκδικος κύριος περὶ πάντων τούτων, καθὼς καὶ προείπαμεν ὑμῖν καὶ διεμαρτυράμεθα.

that no man transgress, and wrong his brother in this matter, because the Lord is an avenger in all these things, as we solemnly forewarned you.

Here Paul deals with the other facet of fornication, namely adultery. Holiness, he says, demands that man does not wrong his brother in this matter (*i.e.*, fornication) by committing sin with his wife. Then the Apostle ends by reminding them of what he had told them in this regard, namely that the Lord will take vengeance on the judgment day (see Rom.

12:18-19) against all those who have committed such sins, *i.e.*, fornication and adultery.

That the sin intended at the beginning of v.6 is adultery, results from the following considerations:

1) The verbs ὑπερβαίνειν and πλεονεκτεῖν appear in the infinitive form and are thus to be understood as object complements of ἰthe verb εἰδέναι in v.4.

2) The definite article τό at the beginning of v.6 emphasizes on the one hand the infinitive form of the two following verbs, while on the other it separates the μή before these verbs and μή in v.5 which logically follows v.4. Consequently τό starts another point in the same logical context.

3) Likewise, the expression ἐν τῷ πράγματι indicates that the Apostle was still dealing with the same topic, namely πορνεία; however, he was speaking here of the wrong done to another brother.

4) Περὶ πάντων τούτων shows that Paul had in mind at least two things.

v.7. οὐ γὰρ ἐκάλεσεν ἡμᾶς ὁ Θεὸς ἐπὶ ἀκαθαρσίᾳ ἀλλ᾽ ἐν ἁγιασμῷ.

For God has not called us for uncleanness, but in holiness.

It was previously shown (see the comments on 2:3) that "ἀκαθαρσία—uncleanness" reflects the heathen way of life, whereas "ἁγιασμός—holiness" is the new state that qualifies the faithful (see the comments on v.3). Thus uncleanness and holiness are in complete opposition. Therefore the Apostle in this verse is saying that God did not call us to stay in the state in which we were, *i.e.*, heathen, but to be transformed into believers, *i.e.*, saints.

Moreover, with Paul the verb "καλέω—to call" usually renders the meaning of the call that took place at baptism, *i.e.*, at our receiving the grace of salvation. This appears in the clearest way in I Cor. 7:17-24: "Only let every one lead

the life which the Lord has assigned to him, and in which
God has called him. This is my rule in all the churches. Was
any one at the time of his call already circumcised? Let
him not seek to remove the marks of circumcision . . . Every
one should remain in the state in which he was called. Were
you a slave when called? Never mind. But if you can gain
your freedom, avail yourself of the opportunity. For he who
was called in the Lord as a slave is a freedman of the Lord.
Likewise he who was free when called is a slave of Christ.
You were bought with a price; do not become slaves of men.
So, brethren, in whatever state each was called, there let him
remain with God." And this is precisely what explains to us
why the Apostle justifies his absolute rejection of fornication
on the grounds of baptism, since in it (read Rom. 6) takes
place the radical change: "For just as you once yielded your
members to impurity and to greater and greater iniquity,
so now yield your members to righteousness for sanctification" (Rom. 6:19).

v.8. τοιγαροῦν ὁ ἀθετῶν οὐκ ἄνθρωπον
ἀθετεῖ ἀλλὰ τὸν Θεὸν τὸν διδόντα
τὸ πνεῦμα αὐτοῦ τὸ ἅγιον εἰς ὑμᾶς.

**Therefore whoever disregards this, disregards
not man but God, who gives His Holy Spirit
to you.**

Paul ends this passage by saying that the sanctification we
were called to in baptism puts us in an immediate relation
with God. Thus, every sin we commit is a slap in God's face,
since the holiness in which we now are is not a human opera-

tion but the direct result of the Holy Spirit's abiding in us.

Therefore our holiness is from that of the Spirit of God, and whenever we fall from it, it is as if we were telling the world that the Holy Spirit is incapable of sanctifying us, *i.e.*, that God has failed to make us share in His glory. Every sin committed by the believers is a setback to God's work!

vv.9-10a. Περὶ δὲ τῆς φιλαδελφείας οὐ χρείαν ἔχετε γράφειν ὑμῖν, αὐτοὶ γὰρ ὑμεῖς θεοδίδακτοί ἐστε εἰς τὸ ἀγαπᾶν ἀλλήλους· καὶ γὰρ ποιεῖτε αὐτὸ εἰς πάντας τοὺς ἀδελφοὺς ἐν ὅλῃ τῇ Μακεδονίᾳ.

But concerning brotherly love you have no need to have any one write to you, for you yourselves have been taught by God to love one another; and indeed you do love all the brethren throughout Macedonia.

The second issue is that of brotherly love and community life. Here again the Apostle states that the Thessalonians are doing very well in showing love toward all the brethren— *i.e.*, all the Christians—in the province of Macedonia. Therefore he does not see the need for further comment. And the reason, he says, is that the Thessalonians are θεοδίδακτοι, *i.e.*, they have been taught by God and have learned from Him. Now this idea is taken from Jeremiah's famous prophecy about the new covenant: "But this is the covenant which I will make with the house of Israel after those days, says the

Lord: I will put my law within them, and I will write it upon their hearts; and I will be their God and they shall be my people. And no longer shall each man teach his neighbor and each brother saying, 'Know the Lord,' for they shall all know me, from the least of them to the greatest, says the Lord; for I will forgive their iniquity, and I will remember their sin no more" (31:33-34).

This is a clear indication that this prophecy was realized, according to Paul, in the community of the brethren where God's law was written upon their hearts through baptism. Thus, this verse confirms that the holy church has been aware from the beginning that she was the community of the last days, *i.e.*, the eschatological community in which all of God's promises are realized.

vv.10b-12. Παρακαλοῦμεν δὲ ὑμᾶς, ἀ-
δελφοί, περισσεύειν μᾶλλον, καὶ
φιλοτιμεῖσθε ἡσυχάζειν καὶ πράσ-
σειν τὰ ἴδια καὶ ἐργάζεσθαι ταῖς
χερσὶν ὑμῶν, καθὼς ὑμῖν παραγ-
γείλαμεν, ἵνα περιπατῆτε εὐσχη-
μόνως πρὸς τοὺς ἔξω καὶ μηδενὸς
χρείαν ἔχητε.

But we exhort you, brethren, to do so more
and more, to aspire to live quietly, to mind
your own affairs, and to work with your hands,
as we charged/instructed you; so that you
may command the respect of outsiders, and
be dependent on nobody.

Although Paul is aware that there was no need for him to write to them concerning brotherly love, yet as apostle and spiritual father he did not miss the opportunity to exhort them to continue and improve on that path. Bu what about manual work, and why did he mention this topic in conjunction with the brotherly love?

It appears from both epistles—especially the second—to the Thessalonians that some of the faithful there thought that the Lord was coming again very soon.[12] These started to see no reason to work for livelihood; they even tried to convince others to follow their way and thus were disturbing the serenity and orderliness of the community life.[13] Further, after some time spent in idleness these people came to be in need of being fed.[14]

Naturally all this made more difficult and even hindered the brotherly love prevailing in the community. Besides, this kind of behavior started to distort the image of God's church in the sight of non-Christians. This is precisely the reason that made Paul not only exhort them to live quietly, to each mind his own affairs and to work with their own hands for livelihood, but even made him instruct, *i.e.*, order them to do so.[15]

v.13. Οὐ θέλομεν δὲ ὑμᾶς ἀγνοεῖν, ἀ-
δελφοί, περὶ τῶν κοιμωμένων, ἵνα

---

[12]This is what made the Apostle emphasize that we are unable to pinpoint the time of the Lord's coming (I Thess. 5:1-2) as well as comment lengthily that there are signs which are to precede that coming (II Thess. 2:1-12).

[13]Note the repetition of the expression "ἀτάκτως περιπατεῖν—behave disorderly" in II Thess. 3, vv.6 and 11.

[14]See especially I Thess. 4:12 and II Thess. 3:10 and 12.

[15]See also II Thess. 3:12.

μὴ λυπῆσθε καθὼς καὶ οἱ λοιποὶ
οἱ μὴ ἔχοντες ἐλπίδα.

But we would not have you ignorant,
brethren, concerning those who are asleep,
that you may not grieve as others do who
have no hope.

The third topic dealt with is in reference to the deceased
Christians. Paul's teachng made it clear that death had no
power any longer over the faithful who will be accompanying
the Lord at His coming in glory. Now doubt had overtaken
some of the Thessalonians, who started asking: If that is
true, then why have some of us died before the Lord's
coming? Does this mean that the deceased will not have a
part in the welcoming procession of the Lord?

The Apostle starts by saying that only non-believers grieve
in the face of death, and the reason for this is that they have
no hope.[16] For the Christian, the heathen is defined as the
one without hope; hence the importance of hope not only
in the life of the faithful, but also in the definition of his
being (refer to the comments on 1:3). The believer is the
one who hopes for victory over death in Christ.

It is to be noted that Paul uses in the verses 13, 14, 15 the
verb "κοιμάομαι—to lie down" when speaking of death. This is
what he will also do in I Cor. 15 in the context of his teaching
regarding our forthcoming resurrection in Christ, where he uses
four times "to lie down" (vv.6, 18, 20 and 51) besides the verb "to
die." With the exception of I Cor. 7:39 and 11:30, these are the
only instances where the verb "to lie down" appears in the Pauline
writings. Now, this use itself is a consolation since it means that
the believer falls asleep in his death awaiting the dashing victory
over death at the Lord's coming. This explains why the terms

---

[16]See also Eph. 2:12.

"κοιμώμενοι—those who are asleep" and "κοιμηθέντες—those who have fallen asleep" to speak of our deceased have made their way into Christian tradition.

v.14. εἰ γὰρ πιστεύομεν ὅτι ᾿Ιησοῦς ἀ-
πέθανεν καὶ ἀνέστη, οὕτως καὶ ὁ
Θεὸς τοὺς κοιμηθέντας διὰ τοῦ
᾿Ιησοῦ ἄξει σὺν αὐτῷ.

For since we believe that Jesus died and rose again, even so, through Jesus, God will bring with him those who have fallen asleep.

The teaching mentioned in the second half of this verse is founded on the content of its first half. It is worthwhile noting that the Apostle does not see any reason to comment on his saying that we believe that Jesus died and rose again. This shows that such a statement expressed a central doctrine of the early church (see our comments on 1:10). "Jesus died and rose again" was for the believers then as well as in subsequent centuries a statement of fact regarding an historical event, which is not only undebatable but also the point of reference for all the other teachings and comments. "Jesus died and rose again" is the cornerstone of the entire theological structure. "Jesus died and rose again": this is what the Christians believe because this is precisely what the apostles preached (see I Cor. 15:1-11, especially v.11).

When Paul comments on the meaning of Christ's resurrection and its consequences for our faith and personal life, he usually prefers the use of either "Christ" or "the Lord" (I Thess. 4:15-18;

Rom. 6:1-12; I Cor. 15:1-29). Therefore his saying here "*Jesus
died and rose again*" is of importance; the emphasis here is on
itself the fact of the resurrection.[17] Indeed the church believed
since the beginning that the historical person Jesus of Nazareth,
son of Mary, is the one who died and rose again; consequently, the
resurrection is not an imaginary event (related to a certain Christ
or Lord) produced by the apostles' zeal resulting from the teachings
of Jesus of Nazareth.

Paul's first epistle to the Thessalonians is the oldest New Testament writing and reflects some facets of the teaching prevailing
in the church less than twenty years after the death of Jesus of
Nazareth on the cross. It is then of utmost importance to note that
in both mentions of the *fact* of the resurrection (1:10 and 4:14)
the Apostle uses the word "Jesus" by itself.

And since the apostles' teaching and the faith of the
church is that those who are asleep in Jesus will share in his
lot[18] (I Cor. 15), it is only logical that God will bring them
in the company of the Lord Jesus at His coming in glory.
In the following verses the Apostle explains how this will
take place.

v.15. Τοῦτο γὰρ ὑμῖν λέγομεν ἐν λόγῳ
κυρίου, ὅτι ἡμεῖς οἱ ζῶντες οἱ περιλειπόμενοι εἰς τὴν παρουσίαν
τοῦ κυρίου οὐ μὴ φθάσωμεν τοὺς
κοιμηθέντας·

For this we declare to you by the word of

---

[17]See for example Acts 2:22: "Jesus the Nazarene/of Nazareth" and
v. 32: "*This* Jesus—τοῦτον τὸν Ἰησοῦν—God raised up, and of that
we are all witnesses."

[18]And this is ultimately the result of the sacrament of baptism, in which
we have all died in Christ (Rom. 6:2-6, 8-9).

the Lord, that we who are alive, who are left
until the coming of the Lord, shall not precede those who have fallen asleep.

Paul's stand concerning the mode of the Second Coming
is founded on a teaching of the Lord Himself. Thus he says
what he says by referring to a word of the Lord.

What is actually meant by the expression "λέγομεν ἐν λόγῳ
κυρίου—we declare by the word of the Lord"? The closest text to
our verse is found in I Cor. 7: "To the married I give charge—
παραγγέλλω—not I but the Lord—οὐκ ἐγὼ ἀλλὰ ὁ κύριος—
that the wife should not separate from her husband . . . and that
the husband should not divorce his wife. To the rest I say, not the
Lord—ἐγώ, οὐχ ὁ κύριος—that if any brother has a wife . . . Now
concerning the unmarried, I have no command of the Lord—
ἐπιταγὴν κυρίου—but I give my opinion as one who by the Lord's
mercy is trustworthy" (vv.10-13 and 25). Hence, the teaching coming from the Lord is either a charge/commandment (v.10 παραγγέλλω) or an order/command (v.25 ἐπιταγή), whereas the
Apostle's teaching is a mere saying (v.12 λέγω). Thus, when
Paul uses in I Thess. 4:15 the expression "we say by the word of
the Lord," he means that what he is writing in this regard is not
a mere opinion but an essential teaching to be heeded by the
Thessalonians.

However, there is no need to be extreme and push to the following
conclusion: Since I Cor. 7:10-11 has its foundation in the teaching of the
Lord Jesus himself,[19] then I Thess. 4:15-17 also goes back to the teaching
of Jesus in Mt. 24:30-31/Mk. 13:25-27. We previously saw during our
comments on 1:6 and 8 that the expression "λόγος κυρίου—the word
of the Lord" meant the gospel that includes the apostles' teaching, i.e., the
teaching of the church concerning Jesus Christ. This is so because the term
"κύριος—Lord" indicates Christ risen from the dead and seated in the
glory of the Father, and who is leading His church on earth until His
coming again (Mt. 28:20).

The content of Paul's teaching regarding the second coming is that those who are alive, i.e., those who will still be

---

[19]See Mt. 5:32/Mk. 10:11-12/Lk. 16:18; Mt. 19:9.

living at the Lord's coming, shall not precede those who
have fallen asleep. This statement exudes a powerful message
of comfort to the Thessalonians since the Apostle is emphasizing that not only the deceased will share in the welcoming
procession for the Lord, but that they will even be *before*
us in the party (see the verses 16 and 17).

vv.16-17. ὅτι αὐτὸς ὁ κύριος ἐν κελεύσμα-
τι, ἐν φωνῇ ἀρχαγγέλου καὶ ἐν
σάλπιγγι Θεοῦ, καταβήσεται ἀπ᾽
οὐρανοῦ, καὶ οἱ νεκροὶ ἐν Χριστῷ
ἀναστήσονται πρῶτον, ἔπειτα ἡ-
μεῖς οἱ ζῶντες οἱ περιλειπόμενοι
ἅμα σὺν αὐτοῖς ἁρπαγησόμεθα ἐν
νεφέλαις εἰς ἀπάντησιν τοῦ κυρίου
εἰς ἀέρα· καὶ οὕτως πάντοτε σὺν
κυρίῳ ἐσόμεθα.

For the Lord himself will descend from
heaven with a cry of command, with the archangel's call and with (the sound of) the trumpet of God. And the dead in Christ will rise
first; then we who are alive, who are left,
shall be caught/snatched up together with
them in the clouds to meet the Lord in the
air; and so we shall always be with the Lord.

The New Testament generally and Paul's epistles particularly
are not comprehensive theological treatises divided in a series of

well designed chapters. It is thus wrong to imagine that these two verses contain the whole of the early church teaching on the coming of the Lord Jesus.[20] The reason is that Paul is usually satisfied with the emphasis on the specific point of importance to his addressees. Now in this our text the Thessalonians are not inquiring about the Lord's coming as such, but rather about the fate of their deceased relatives and friends; consequently the Apostle's answer is restricted to that. Note that v.16 begins with "ὅτι—for/since/because" which is a causal conjunction and thus is explanatory of the preceding. And *the point in v.15 is* not the Lord's coming, but *that we* who are left until His coming *shall not precede those* who have *fallen asleep*.

In this description of the Lord's parousia, Paul uses biblical images common in the rendering of theophanies. One such image is the sound of the trumpet, which is a common usage among many people since remote times and until our own days.[21] As for the trumpet sounding, it is the office of the angels;[22] hence the parallelism between the archangel's call and the trumpet of God.[23] Yet the aim of the trumpet sounding is twofold: it announces the arrival of the king or governor or victorious general on the one hand, while on the other it reminds the populace or the citizens that they have to proceed toward the welcoming of the honored visitor.[24] This last aspect explains the use of κέλευσμα, whose meaning is "command/order."[25] Thus the voice of the trumpeting archangel will announce the coming of the Lord Himself, yet it will also carry an order to His welcoming party to get ready in order to receive their Lord coming to them as victor. The element of victory is reflected in that the Lord Jesus

---

[20]In order to comprehend the whole of the early church's teaching in this matter we would have to study *all* of the New Testament passages pertaining to this topic.

[21]For example the siren of the police in official motorcades.

[22]Mt. 24:31; Rev. 8:2.

[23]See Rev. 10:7. Compare also Rev. 1:10 and 4:1.

[24]See Appendix V on παρουσία.

[25]The translation "cry of command" renders the parallelism of κέλευσμα with the other two expressions: the archangel's call and the trumpet of God.

will descend from heaven where He is abiding in divine glory after His victory over death (see 1:10). As to the party of Jesus, it will include two kinds of people: (a) those who died in Christ, *i.e.*, those faithful who are deceased, and (b) us the believers who are still alive. Therefore the result of the trumpet sounding will be twofold: "first—πρῶτον" the dead in Christ will rise, and "then—ἔπειτα" we shall be caught up *together with them* (ἅμα σὺν αὐτοῖς) to meet the Lord. Paul makes it thus clear to the Thessalonians that there is no need to grieve since both our deceased and we are in the same position in regard to the coming of the Lord Jesus.

To say that the dead in Christ will rise without dealing with the destiny of the sinners is another indication of what was asserted earlier, namely that Paul's intention here is not to present a comprehensive teaching or a full study of a subject entitled: The Lord's Coming, the Last Resurrection and the Final Judgment. His aim is rather to comfort the Thessalonians. This is further reflected in: (a) the use of the temporal adverbs "πρῶτον—first" and "ἔπειτα—then," as well as (b) the use of the preposition "ἅμα—together, at the same time" along with the preposition "σὺν—with" before the pronoun "αὐτοῖς—them."

Now the mode of the Lord's encounter is rendered by Paul as a snatching. The verb "ἁρπάζομαι—to be snatched up, to be caught up" appears only twice more in his writings, and both times when speaking of the Lord Jesus' appearance to him on the road to Damascus. Thus he writes in II Cor. 12 that he was caught up to the third heaven (v.2) and to heaven (v.3). It is quite clear then that the use of this verb by Paul is restricted to those situations whereby man is taken from this our tangible world into God's world.[26] This indicates that the Apostle is well aware of the radical dif-

---

[26]This verb is found a fourth time in the New Testament only in Rev. 12:5, which reads: "but her child was caught/snatched up to God and to his throne."

ference between the mode of the Lord's coming on the one hand and that of the coming of an earthly king or ruler on the other. Thus we will not go or walk or move to meet the Lord, but we will be snatched up (and the snatching is a divine action!) to Him. Now this snatching up will be of a similar nature or kind as that of the Lord's coming itself: we shall be caught up "in the clouds—ἐν νεφέλαις" upon which he will be coming.[27] In biblical usage the cloud accompanies God's epiphanies and in it we meet Him (Mt. 17:5/Mk. 9:7/Lk. 9:34-35). He abides in it, and it is a sign of His glory (see our comments on 2:13). As to the air, it is where the clouds are and thus is the place which is beyond our earthly world. Finally, this meeting will bring us into being always in the company of the Lord, and that in the eternal glory and life-giving presence of God.

All the preceding means that verses 16 and 17 are a rendering in imagery (based on traditional images and expressions taken from the Old Testament as well as the Apostle's contemporary world) of what Paul has already said in v.14. Indeed:

1) The teaching presented as the word of the Lord (vv.15-17) is linked to the preceding (v.14 *only*) with the explanatory conjunction "γάρ—for, since." Note that v.14 is in its turn connected to v.13 through another γάρ. Also note that the passage vv.15-17 flows without any interruption by any of the particles common in the Pauline writings: "γάρ—since, for," "δέ—as for" or "οὖν—thus, therefore."

2) The idea with which Paul concludes v.17 is identical to the conclusion of v.14, namely: the believers in Jesus will end by being with Him in His glory. Observe the parallelism between the statement that God will bring—ἄξει—those who have fallen asleep and the fact that we shall be caught up—ἁρπαγησόμεθα (here also the doer is God!). Also observe that both v.14 and vv.15-17 end with the same point: "with him (*i.e.*, Jesus)—σὺν αὐτῷ" and "with the Lord—σὺν κυρίῳ."

Practically speaking all this means that one ought not to overdo

---

[27]Mt. 24:30/Mk. 13:26/Lk. 21:27; Mt. 26:64/Mk. 14:62; Rev. 1:7; 14:14. See also Acts 1:9.

the issue of understanding the mode of the general resurrection since it is after all a divine action similar to a certain extent with the resurrection of the Lord Jesus. Now it is known fact that we do not find in any of the four canonical Gospels a description of the event of Jesus' resurrection from the dead. What should rather be stressed is that at the general resurrection we shall be in the company of the Lord Jesus in God's glory, and that, "πάντοτε—always," *i.e.*, for good. This should make us not worry about anything else since Jesus is our heaven! Indeed, the whole resurrection will be a vain operation if it does not end with what the Apostle said: ". . . and so we shall always be with the Lord!"

v.18. Ὥστε παρακαλεῖτε ἀλλήλους ἐν τοῖς λόγοις τούτοις.

Therefore comfort (and strengthen) each other with these words.

Paul finishes this passage (vv.13-18) by asking the Thessalonians to comfort and strengthen[28] one another with the teaching he has just left them with. Now such a teaching is indeed capable of consoling and strengthening since it is "by the word of the Lord—ἐν λόγῳ κυρίου" (v.15).

---

[28]The verb παρακαλέω carries both meanings: refer to our comments on 3:2.

CHAPTER FIVE

Περὶ δὲ τῶν χρόνων καὶ τῶν και-
ρῶν, ἀδελφοί, οὐ χρείαν ἔχετε ὑμῖν
γράφεσθαι, αὐτοὶ γὰρ ἀκριβῶς οἴδατε ὅτι ἡμέρα κυρίου ὡς κλέπτης
ἐν νυκτὶ οὕτως ἔρχεται.

But as to the times and the seasons, brethren,
you have no need to have anything written to
you. For you yourselves know well that the
day of the Lord will come like a thief in the
night.

With that, Paul proceeds to a fourth topic (somehow
related to the previous one), namely: the time of the Lord's
coming. The expression "the times and the seasons—χρόνοι
καὶ καιροί" was common in the early church; it meant the
indicated moments for specific events in the course of God's
design.[1] Consequently they are absolutely in God's hand
(Acts 1:7 and 17:26) and no one can know them except
He (Acts 1:7).

The Apostle starts by saying that there is no need for
the Thessalonians to receive any further comment in this re-

---

[1] Compare Mt. 8:29; 16:3; 26:18; Mk. 1:15; Lk. 1:20; 4:13; 21:8, 24;
Jn. 7:6, 8; Acts 1:7; 17:26; Rom. 5:6; Eph. 1:10; I Tim. 2:6; Tit. 1:3.

gard, since they know but too well the church's teaching in this matter: the day of the Lord will come like a thief in the night. And a thief does not inform anyone of the hour of his arrival (Mt. 24:43 / Lk. 12:39).

What might be the origin of this imagery: the day of the Lord will come like a thief in the night? The expression "day of the Lord" is used by the Old Testament prophets in reference to the day on which God appears to judge men. Now this day comes always at an unexpected moment. And Jesus did say: "Watch therefore, for you do not know on what day your Lord is coming. But know this, that if the householder had known in what part of the night the thief was coming, he would have watched and would not have let his house be broken into. Therefore you also must be ready; for the son of man is coming at an hour you do not expect" (Mt. 24:42-44; see also Lk. 12:38-40); John the seer has kept this tradition in his book: Jesus will come like a thief, be awake (Rev. 3:3 and 16:15).

However, in another ramification of the tradition, the image of the thief passed in its application from the Lord Himself to His day, as we read in II Pet. 3:10 and in our text here. The proof that this aspect of the tradition goes back to the same source, namely Jesus Himself, is found in the fact that Paul compares the day of the Lord to a thief coming in the night, which is exactly what we find in Matthew and Luke.[2]

v.3. ὅταν λέγωσιν, Εἰρήνη καὶ ἀσφάλεια, τότε αἰφνίδιος αὐτοῖς ἐφίσταται ὄλεθρος ὥσπερ ἡ ὠδὶν τῇ ἐν
γαστρὶ ἐχούσῃ, καὶ οὐ μὴ ἐκφύγω-
σιν.

When people say, "There is peace and se-

---

[2]Notice that some manuscripts add the expression "in the night" in II Pet. 3:10.

curity," then sudden destruction will come upon them as travail comes upon a woman with
child, and there will be no escape.

We have translated this verse as a general truth (and not as if it were
referring to a specific future event) for the following reasons:

1) Such a translation follows the rules of Greek syntax: the main verb
is in the present indicative (ἐφίσταται),[3] whereas the subordinate one is
in the present subjunctive (λέγωσιν).

2) The subject in the main phrase ὄλεθρος is indefinite.

3) This verse follows the preceding one without any of the conjunc-
tions δέ, γάρ, οὖν, nor even the coordinating καί. It thus seems to be
a comment by Paul on his statement that the day of the Lord will come
like a thief in the night.

4) In the following verses 4-11, Paul does not use any of the terms
appearing in this our verse. He rather resumes the thought expressed in
v.2. (Note the use of ἡμέρα and κλέπτης in v.4; note also the use of
σκότος in v.4 which is a parallel term to νύξ as it appears from v.5.)
Thus v.3 sounds like a parenthesis full of quotations well known from
the Scriptures, whereby the Apostle intended to emphasize the suddenness
of the coming of the Lord's day.

The absence of any of the terms appearing in v.3 from the rest
of the passage 5:1-11 is a clear proof that it is meant as a support-
ing quote. The question is: What are the sources of this quotation?

The two terms "peace—εἰρήνη" and "security—ἀσφάλεια" are
found in a similar context neither in the Pauline writings nor
in the rest of the New Testament. As to the Old Testament, our
only source is the prophet Jeremiah who says in a context very
similar[4] to our text the following: ". . . saying: 'Peace, peace' when
there is no peace" (6:14/8:11). Observe the repetition "peace,
peace" as compared to the wording in our verse: "peace and security."[5]

Here are some statistical data regarding the second half of v.3:

1) The adjective "αἰφνίδιος—sudden" appears only here at

---

[3]Notice that the verb ἔρχεται in v.2 is also in the present and not the
future.

[4]Jer. 6:12-15/8:10-12.

[5]The repetition of the same word for the sake of emphasis is common
in the Semitic languages, whereas Greek prefers the use of two synonymous
or comparable words.

Paul's hand, while it is found one other time in a passage about the Lord's Coming (*Lk. 21:34*).[6]

2) Likewise the verb "ἐφίστημι—to come upon" appears only here in the Pauline epistles and once more (*Lk. 21:34*) with the same meaning in a passage about the Lord's coming.

3) The word "ὄλεθρος—destruction" is found here and in II Thess. 1:9 and I Tim. 6:9.[7]

4) The term "ὠδὶν—travail" appears here and in Mt. 24:8/ Mk. 13:8.[8]

5) We meet the expression "ἐν γαστρὶ ἔχουσα—with child" only here and in Mt. 24:19/Mk. 13:17/*Lk. 21:23*, in the same context.

6) The idea of fleeing because of the hardship due to the Lord's coming is encountered in Mt. 24:16/Mk. 13:14/*Lk. 21:21* and Mt. 24:20. Add to this that we find the same verb ἐκφεύγω in *Lk. 21:36*.

These data clearly show that Paul's source is the early church tradition that conveyed to us the teaching of Jesus Christ about the suddenness and the hardship of the last days. Observe especially the close similarity between I Thess. 5:2-3 and the tradition preserved in Luke.

Having said—according to the teaching of Jesus[9]—that the Lord's day will come as a thief in the night, Paul digresses to include a comment he takes also from the Master's teaching about the last days,[10]: when the people say "peace and security,"[11] *i.e.*, everything is fine, the Lord will come suddenly as travail comes upon a pregnant woman, and His day will be a day of great desolation since the people will not be able to find a way out.

---

[6]In Mk. 13:36 (which is parallel to Lk. 21:34) we have the temporal adverb ἐξαίφνης.

[7]The fourth instance is in I Cor. 5:5, but the context is different.

[8]The fourth instance is in Acts 2:24, but the context is different.

[9]See our comments on the previous verse.

[10]See at least Lk. 21:21, 23, 34, 36.

[11]See Jer. 6:14/8:11 and Ez. 13:10.

vv.4-5. ὑμεῖς δέ, ἀδελφοί, οὐκ ἐστὲ ἐν
σκότει, ἵνα ἡ ἡμέρα ὑμᾶς ὡς κλέπτης καταλάβῃ, πάντες γὰρ ὑμεῖς
υἱοὶ φωτὸς ἐστὲ καὶ υἱοὶ ἡμέρας.
οὐκ ἐσμὲν νυκτὸς οὐδὲ σκότους.

But you are not in darkness, brethren, for
that day to surprise/come upon you like a
thief. For you are all sons of light and sons
of the day; we are not of the night or of
darkness.

The theme of the suddenness of the Lord's day and the
predicament in which it puts those unprepared urges the
Apostle to exhort the Thessalonians to be awake and watchful during the period of waiting. Striking in this respect is
that Paul uses the mention of the *day* of the Lord—ἡμέρα
κυρίου[12]—coming in the *night*—νυκτί—to clothe his exhortation with an imagery common in the Scriptures, namely:
the opposition between light and darkness, day and night.[13]
Thus he starts by saying that what was mentioned in v.3
will not apply to the faithful because they are not in darkness (*i.e.*, they are in the light), and consequently the Lord's
day will not come upon (*i.e.*, surprise) them as a thief as
it does upon those who do not expect it. Then Paul underlines that all—πάντες—the faithful are children of light
and children of the day. He then ends by including himself
with them (ἐσμέν) when he says: Since we are children of

[12c]Ἡμέρα like "day" in English has the meaning of daytime (as opposed to night) as well as that of a twenty-four hour period.

[13]Compare with Rom. 2:19; 13:12-13; I Cor. 4:5; II Cor. 4:6; 6:14;
Eph. 5:8, 11; Col. 1:13.

light and of the day, we do not pertain to the night nor
to darkness, nor are we related in any way to them.

Observe that "ἡ ἡμέρα—the day" is alone with the definite article
and thus means the Lord's day, whereas the other terms (darkness, light,
day, night) in vv.4-8 are indefinite and thus are part of Paul's imagery
to render the radical difference between the children of light and those
of darkness. Therefore one should not understand the expression υἱοὶ ἡμέρας
of v.5 (and ἡμέρας ὄντες in v.8) in the sense of sons of the Lord's day,
but rather in that of sons of the day, i.e., of the light.

vv.6-7. ἄρα οὖν μὴ καθεύδωμεν ὡς οἱ
λοιποί, ἀλλὰ γρηγορῶμεν καὶ νή-
φωμεν· οἱ γὰρ καθεύδοντες νυκτὸς
καθεύδουσιν, καὶ οἱ μεθυσκόμενοι
νυκτὸς μεθύουσιν.

So then let us not sleep, as the others do,
but let us keep awake and be sober. For those
who sleep, sleep at night, and those who get
drunk are drunk at night.

The result of that which the Apostle said in vv.4-5 is
obvious: the others, i.e., the non-believers,[14] do not heed
the Lord's coming and thus they sleep during the period of
waiting (i.e., the night). As for us, we must not sleep; yet,
not sleeping here does not mean only keeping awake (γρηγορῶμεν) but complete soberness (νήφωμεν) also. Why?
Because there are two kinds of children of night, i.e., darkness: some sleep, but others stay up and get drunk! Therefore
staying awake is not at all enough to make us children of

[14]This is the meaning of "οἱ λοιποί—the others." See our comments on
4:13.

the light and the day, but we ought to be watchful and fully
sober lest we fall in sin. Thus the important thing during
our awaiting the Lord's coming is *sinlessness*. That this is
obviously the intention of the Apostle himself is shown in
that, at the conclusion of his recommendations in this
matter, he says in v.8: "νήφωμεν—let us be sober" without
any mention of keeping awake.

It is to be noted that the idea of staying awake on the one hand
and that of soberness on the other are mentioned in the gospels of
Matthew, Mark and Luke in an identical context to that in which
they appear in vv.2-3 here at Paul's hand:
= staying awake and watchful: Mt. 24:42/Mk. 13:35; Mt.
24:43/Lk. 12:39;[15] Mk. 13:34, 37; Lk. 12:37; add also Mk. 13:33/
Lk. 21:36 where we find the verb "ἀγρυπνεῖτε" which has the
same meaning as γρηγορεῖτε.
= soberness/drunkenness: Mt. 24:49/Lk. 12:45; Lk. 21:34; see
also Mt. 24:38/Lk. 17:27; Lk. 17:28.
All this confirms what has been said before: that Paul took his
imagery in this passage on the last days from the stock of church
tradition which kept the teaching of Jesus Christ in this regard and
which we encounter in detail in the synoptic gospels.

v.8. ἡμεῖς δὲ ἡμέρας ὄντες νήφωμεν, ἐν-
δυσάμενοι θώρακα πίστεως καὶ ἀ-
γάπης καὶ περικεφαλαίαν ἐλπίδα
σωτηρίας.

But, since we belong to day, let us be sober,
and put on the breastplate of faith and love,
and for a helmet the hope of salvation.

Now if the children of the night get drunk, then sober-

---

[15]Not in all manuscripts, for Lk. 12:39.

ness is the sign of the children of the day. And as we have seen, the aim of this soberness is not to fall in sin. However, such a stand is not possible unless we get ready for the battle, for the powers of the evil one are all around us trying to make us fall by not awaiting hopefully any longer the Lord's coming. The aggressiveness of the devil's attack against us is reflected in the fact that both the breastplate and the helmet[16] are defensive weapons that help us withstand attacks and keep our position. As for the breastplate, it is our faith in Jesus Christ and our love towards the brethren, while the helmet is our hope in the salvation brought to us by the Lord on His day.[17]

vv.9-10. ὅτι οὐκ ἔθετο ἡμᾶς ὁ Θεὸς εἰς ὀργὴν ἀλλὰ εἰς περιποίησιν σωτηρίας διὰ τοῦ κυρίου ἡμῶν Ἰησοῦ Χριστοῦ, τοῦ ἀποθανόντος ὑπὲρ ἡμῶν ἵνα εἴτε γρηγορῶμεν εἴτε καθεύδωμεν ἅμα σὺν αὐτῷ ζήσωμεν.

For God has not destined us for wrath, but to obtain salvation through our Lord Jesus Christ, who died for us so that whether we wake or sleep we might live with him.

The necessity for our continuous awakenness stems from that God's intention and design for us is not damnation on

---

[16]The image is taken from Is. 59:17.
[17]Refer to our comments on 1:3 for a detailed study on the three virtues of faith, love and hope.

the day of His coming wrath (see 1:10), but the obtaining of the salvation secured for us by Jesus Christ. Now this was realized in that Jesus died for our sake so that we might live with Him in His resurrection, since this is salvation: that we live together with the Lord who overcame death.

At the end of his words regarding the suddenness of the Lord's coming, the Apostle remembers the Thessalonians' worry about their deceased (4:13-18). Therefore he emphasizes that the Lord's death happened for us *all*, whether we wake or sleep—*i.e.*, whether we are alive or dead—so that we *all* live together with Him.

Our understanding of "whether we wake or sleep" as meaning "whether we are alive or dead" is founded on the following two points:

1) If the emphasis in this passage were only on the fact that we will live with Christ, the Apostle would have been satisfied with saying "σὺν αὐτῷ—with Him" as he did in 4:17b (σὺν κυρίῳ—with the Lord). But the inclusion of "ἅμα—together" before it takes us back to ἅμα of 4:17a (ἅμα σὺν αὐτοῖς—together with them) where the emphasis is on the reunion of the Thessalonians with their deceased at the Lord's coming.

2) To consider some of the believers to be sleeping in the sense of this word in vv.6-7 would create an insurmountable contradiction between v.10 and vv.6-8.

But the question remains: why did the Apostle use this figurative way of speech and not simply say "whether we are alive or dead"? We believe the reasons to be the following:

1) The overall intended point of the entire passage 5:2-9 is that the believers ought to remain awake.

2) If Paul had used "εἴτε ζῶμεν—whether we live/are alive," there would have been a repetition with "ζήσωμεν—we might live" at the end of the verse.

3) The use of ζήσωμεν instead of "ἀναστήσωμεν—we might rise/be raised" after "τοῦ ἀποθανόντες—who died" can be explained by the fact that, in 4:16-17, the Apostle had said that only the dead would rise (before their snatching up) while the living would be snatched up.

v.11. Διὸ παρακαλεῖτε ἀλλήλους καὶ
οἰκοδομεῖτε εἰς τὸν ἕνα, καθὼς καὶ
ποιεῖτε.

Therefore encourage/comfort one another
and build/edify one another up, just as you
are doing.

Coming back to the idea that both dead and living will
be together with the risen Lord (similar to that found in
4:17), Paul finishes his second point regarding the parousia
(*viz.*, we do not know its time, thus let us be soberly awake:
5:1-10) with the same exhortation with which he ended his
first point (*viz.*, the deceased will be present at the Lord's
coming: 4:13-17), namely: "encourage/comfort one another—παρακαλεῖτε ἀλλήλους" (see 4:18). However,
the Apostle adds here the idea of "building—οἰκοδομεῖτε"
one another. The notion that the church of Christ, the community of the believers, is a building growing on the basis
of mutual edification will be treated extensively by Paul in
his subsequent letters. It is worthwhile to simply note at
this point that here again the Apostle shows that another
one of his central ideas was part of his theology already
at this early stage of his life. Subsequent experiences seem
to have enriched his vision but not to have changed it.

vv. 12-13. ᾽Ερωτῶμεν δὲ ὑμᾶς, ἀδελφοί,
εδέναι τοὺς κοπιῶντας ἐν ὑμῖν καὶ
προϊσταμένους ὑμῶν ἐν κυρίῳ καὶ
νουθετοῦντας ὑμᾶς, καὶ ἡγεῖσθαι

αὐτοὺς ὑπερεκπερισσοῦ ἐν ἀγάπῃ
διὰ τὸ ἔργον αὐτῶν· εἰρηνεύετε ἐν
ἑαυτοῖς.

We demand of you, brethren, to acknowl-
edge/respect those who labor among you and
are over you/leaders in the Lord and ad-
monish/reprove you, and to esteem them very
highly in love because of their work. Be at
peace among yourselves.

At the end of his letter the Apostle gives some practical
advice pertaining to the community life of the church, starting with the respect and esteem owed to the leaders. Though
their office asks of them admonition and sometimes even
reproof, nevertheless this their leadership is in the Lord and
what they accomplish they do in His name and under His
inspiration. Now this is clear in that they labor and tire
more than the rest of the faithful, since their work imposes
on them a continual watch over the life of the church. The
believers are even asked to esteem them very highly by
expressing their love toward them, since after all these are
only fulfilling their duty. Then Paul finishes by asking that
peace—God's peace (see 1:1)—reign among them so that
they be a good example for the outsiders (see 4:12).

Note that the Apostle starts his presentation of the church leaders
by saying that they work, labor and tire; then he mentions that
they are at the head of the community—and this at any rate "ἐν
κυρίῳ—in the Lord"; and only lastly he says that they admonish/
reprove. Notice also that he finishes his demand by coming back
to the mention of "their work—ἔργον αὐτῶν," affirming that
this is the reason for his requesting the faithful to love and respect
them "ὑπερεκπερισσοῦ—very highly." Notice finally the emphasis[18]

---

[18]The verb εἰρηνεύετε is in the imperative and thus reflects the

on the importance of peace (being at peace with each other) in
the life of the community. Add to the aforementioned the fact that
the fourfold request in v.14 starts with asking that the "unruly—
ἀτάκτους" brethren be reproved.

All this might well indicate that those who were idle have
disturbed the "order—τάξις" in the life of the church,[19] and that
they have even started a kind of rebellion against the leaders who
had tried to discipline them. Now such a disorder could weaken
the church and make her an object of scorn for both Jews and
Gentiles. This would, in our opinion, explain the bringing up again
of this subject after having dealt with it in 4:9-12 when the Apostle
was picking up some of the points which Timothy had drawn to his
attention (4:1-5:11).[20]

v.14. Παρακαλοῦμεν δὲ ὑμᾶς, ἀδελφοί, νουθετεῖτε τοὺς ἀτάκτως, πα-
ραμυθεῖσθε τοὺς ὀλιγοψύχους,
ἀντέχεσθε τῶν ἀσθενῶν, μακρο-
θυμεῖτε πρὸς πάντας.

And we exhort you brethren, admonish/
reprove the unruly, encourage the fainthearted, help the weak, be patient with
(them) all.

See our comment in 4:1 regarding the differences between ἐρωτῶμεν
and παρακαλοῦμεν.

After having finished with the topic of the behavior of

idea of a powerful request (almost an order) between the command (v.12)
and the exhortation (v.14).
[19]See I Thess. 4:11-12 and II Thess. 3:6-15.
[20]Notice also that the Apostle's prayer of v.23 is addressed to the God
of peace.

the faithful toward their leaders in the church, the Apostle
issues some directives in regard to the general stand of the
believers toward their brethren: admonish and even reprove
those who behave against the order of community life and
transgress the basic instructions; strengthen and encourage
the fainthearted for whatever reason (persecution, difficulty
of Christian life, the belatedness of the Lord's coming...);
help the weak in faith or in body; as for patience, it is to be
exercised toward all the brethren.[21]

v.15. ὁρᾶτε μή τις κακὸν ἀντὶ κακοῦ
τινι ἀποδῷ, ἀλλὰ πάντοτε ἀγα-
θὸν διώκετε εἰς ἀλλήλους καὶ εἰς
πάντας.

See that none of you repays evil for evil,
but always seek to do good to one another
and to all.

Paul ends his practical instructions concerning community
life by asking the Thessalonians not to repay evil for evil,
but that the common good be their goal in their dealing with
all the brethren. This his request bears the tone of cautioning
(ὁρᾶτε—see), for the Apostle knows only too well that the
devil is the one who incites to evil. Human nature usually
renders evil for evil, and such an attitude triggers a vicious
cycle of reactions that culminate with the destruction of
community life and thus the ultimate winner will be the devil
himself, since his ultimate aim is to damage the edifice (see

[21]See I Cor. 13:4 and Gal. 5:22.

v.11: οἰκοδομεῖτε—build) that the Lord builds up, namely
the church. Therefore, hindering the progress of evil whenever it gets to us is a slap in the devil's face and a victory
for God's saving work.[22]

vv.16-18. Πάντοτε χαίρετε, ἀδιαλείπτως προσεύχεσθε, ἐν παντὶ εὐχα-
ριστεῖτε· τοῦτο γὰρ θέλημα Θεοῦ
ἐν Χριστῷ Ἰησοῦ εἰς ὑμᾶς.

Rejoice always, pray constantly, give thanks in
all circumstances; for this is the will of God
in Christ Jesus for you.

Paul has taught us in 1:6 that true joy is a gift of the
Holy Spirit and therefore it totally fills the life of the faithful (2:19-20 and 3:9). Therefore he starts his last set of
instructions (vv. 16-22) by saying: "Rejoice always." Grief
is indeed the sign of the non-believer (4:13); as for the
faithful, he knows that victory is to God and to all those
who love Him. Still, joy might leave us if we do not nurture
it through a continual relationship with God, the cause of
our joy; hence the Apostle's request: "Pray constantly," *i.e.*,
do not miss praying at the given daily times.

We know that the early church was much influenced in her
prayer life by Judaic customs; now in Jewish tradition the assigned
daily prayers were three. Therefore, the immediate meaning of the
Apostle's words is the perseverance in these assigned daily prayers.

---

[22]See the comparable passage of Rom. 12:17-21.

Yet Paul's request ends thus: "Give thanks in all circumstances." We have said in 1:3 that thanksgiving was an
essential aspect of prayer,[23] which means that we are not to
restrict our prayer life to those given times of the day, but
we take every possible opportunity to give thanks to God
for His everlasting grace that fills us with joy (see 3:9). If
we are to rejoice always, then we must give thanks at all
times! That is, according to the Apostle, God's will for us
in Jesus Christ.

In the Pauline writings God's will means His intention
for us and His saving design which He realized in Jesus
Christ.[24] Thus constant joy and thanksgiving are, in Paul's eyes,
two factors pertaining to the essence of mission, since in them
are mirrored both our immutable faith that the Lord Jesus
has conquered death which provokes grief, as well as our
call to the others to join our ranks.

vv.19-22. τὸ πνεῦμα μὴ σβέννυτε, προφη-
τείας μὴ ἐξουθενεῖτε· πάντα δὲ δο-
κιμάζετε, τὸ καλὸν κατέχετε, ἀπὸ
παντὸς εἴδους πονηροῦ ἀπέχεσθε.

Do not extinguish/quench the Spirit, do not
despise prophesying, but test everything;
hold fast what is good, abstain from every
form of evil.

Paul's second instruction deals with the gift of prophecy
in the early church (read carefully I Cor. 12 and 14). He

---

[23]See 2:13 where the Apostle gives thanks "ἀδιαλείπτως—unceasingly."
[24]Compare 4:3.

advises that the church prophets be not despised, since exhortation, comfort and encouragement are their main duty (I Cor. 14:3 and 31). The importance of the office of prophecy appears clearly from the text of our epistle where the verb παρακαλῶ and the noun παράκλησις are mentioned nine times in five small chapters. Now, despising prophecy might lead to the quenching of the Holy Spirit in the life of the church, since prophecy is one of his main gifts. Indeed, it comes in the second place after apostleship (I Cor. 12:28), and Paul has exhorted the faithful to aspire for it (I Cor. 14:1 and 39).

However, this does not mean that the Thessalonians are to accept any kind of prophecies, but they ought to test and search them (see I Jn. 4:1), then to hold fast what is good, namely every prophecy that aims at the common good (see our comments on v.15). As for the prophecies that do not originate in God's Spirit, they are of the evil kind, and the faithful ought to abstain from them.

vv.23-24. Αὐτὸς ὁ Θεὸς τῆς εἰρήνης ἁγιάσαι ὑμᾶς ὁλοτελεῖς, καὶ ὁλόκληρον ὑμῶν τὸ πνεῦμα καὶ ἡ ψυχὴ καὶ τὸ σῶμα ἀμέμπτως ἐν τῇ παρουσίᾳ τοῦ κυρίου ἡμῶν Ἰησοῦ Χριστοῦ τηρηθείη. πιστὸς ὁ καλῶν ὑμᾶς, ὃς καὶ ποιήσει.

May the God of peace himself sanctify you wholly; and may your spirit and soul and body in their totality be kept without blame

at the coming of our Lord Jesus Christ. He
who calls you is faithful, and He will do it.

The word "peace—εἰρήνη" renders the atmosphere of
the kingdom where all God's promises (see our comments
on 1:1) are realized, and holiness is the basic condition to
enter therein (see 4:3-7). Consequently, as he has previously
beseeched the Lord to keep the hearts of the Thessalonians
"unblamable in holiness—ἀμέμπτους ἐν ἀγιωσύνῃ," Paul
repeats at the end of the letter his prayer that God sanctify
them wholly (ἀγιάσαι ὁλοτελεῖς).[25] Moreover this his
prayer is addressed to the God of peace Himself, since He
is the Lord of the kingdom and He alone can sanctify the
people in a full way that allows them to enter it. And holiness means that every faithful be kept in his totality (ὁλόκληρον)—that is: spirit, soul and body—blameless at the
coming of the Lord Jesus.

Finally, He who calls us, *i.e.,* God (see 2:12 and 4:7)—
and His calling is to holiness (4:7)!—is faithful to His
calling and promise; therefore, He will actualize Paul's
petition. The Apostle's intention is clear here: to comfort and
strengthen the Thessalonians.

The main difficulty in v.23 lies in that we find only here at
Paul's hand (indeed, in the entire New Testament) the human
being in three parts: spirit, soul and body. Therefore, this text has
presented a kind of an enigma to the interpreters. Following are
some considerations to help solve it:

1) The biblical view of man is that he is not out of two parts,
but one unit with two faces: the soul—ψυχή—and the body—σῶμα.
The first represents the vitality of the latter, while the second is
the tangible and practical base of the former. Therefore we never
find in the Pauline writings the soul as opposed to the body, rather
each one of them expresses the totality of man.

---

[25]Note the use of the verb "ἀμέμπτως—without blame" at the end of
the verse.

2) On the other hand the word "spirit" is also another expression for "man."[26] However, Paul uses it to indicate human life on the level of thought, understanding, feelings, behavior, *etc.*: all aspects of humanity in man. Thus our spirit is the center where we meet the Spirit of God, and the Apostle did compare the one with the other.[27]

3) The fruits of the work of God's Spirit in us are at odds with our actions resulting from sin, on the one hand; our "spirit" is but the opening through which the Holy Spirit is poured into our lives and works in us, on the other. Paul therefore sometimes uses the word "spirit" in opposition to either "the soul"[28] or "the body."[29]

Consequently, we believe that the correct reading of v.23 is not: your spirit//and soul//and body (that is, separating the three), nor: your spirit and soul//and body (that is, separating the first two on the one hand, and the third on the other), but rather: your spirit//and soul and body (that is, separating the spirit on the one hand, and the soul with the body on the other).

But then, why did the Apostle not simply mention either "the soul" or "the body" in parallel with the expression "spirit," but include both words? The answer lies in the fact that the two adjectives "ὁλοτελεῖς—total, whole" and "ὁλόκληρον—complete, full" appear only here in all of Paul's letters.[30] The use of both words at once by the Apostle and in the same verse—although they bear the same meaning—is a clear indication that the writer intended to emphasize a point, namely the totality.[31] Thus Paul's prayer is that God keep the believers *whole/complete* in holiness and *totally/ fully* without blame until the coming of the Lord Jesus. It is as if he was asking God to preserve *everything* in each one of the faithful. And this thought carried him to write "soul and body" along with "spirit," *i.e.*, to use all of the possible words[32] that rendered the meaning of human being.

---

[26]I Cor. 5:4; 14:14; 16:18; II Cor. 2:13; 7:13; Gal. 4:23; Phil. 1:27.

[27]Rom. 8:9-11; 8:16; I Cor. 2:11.

[28]I Cor. 15:45.

[29]Rom. 8:10, 11, 13b; I Cor. 5:3/Col. 2:5.

[30]As for the rest of the New Testament, the former is not encountered at all, while the latter is found only once in James 1:4.

[31]Notice that both adjectives are compound, where in both cases the first part ὅλος means "all, the whole of, the totality of."

[32]With the exception of "σάρξ—flesh," which is usually, according to the Apostle Paul, the center of sin in the human being.

v.25. Ἀδελφοί, προσεύχεσθε καὶ περὶ ἡμῶν.

Brethren, pray for us as well.

Then Paul asks the Thessalonians to pray also for him
(and his companions), that God may keep him (them)
wholly blameless at/until the Lord's coming.

We have opted for the manuscripts which read "καὶ—and/also/as well"
between προσεύχεσθε and περὶ ἡμῶν, against those that omit it, for the
following reasons:

1) It is definitely the more difficult reading (*lectio difficilior*). Why
would a copyist add καί, especially since it is not found in II Thess. 3:1a
where we have the same wording: προσεύχεσθε, ἀδελφοί, περὶ ἡμῶν?
On the other hand, copyists would omit it (perhaps under the influence
of II Thess. 3:1) assuming that there is no need here for an "as well/also."

2) The parallel II Thess. 3:1a is in a context (vv.1-5) similar to that of
I Thess. 5:23-24, namely that of the parousia. Indeed:

(a) Notice the use of πιστὸς δέ ἐστιν ὁ κύριος in II Thess. 3:3,
which is parallel to πιστὸς ὁ καλῶν ὑμᾶς of I Tess. 5:24;

(b) The aim of the prayer asked for by Paul is that the word of the
Lord, *i.e.*, the gospel, be successful where he is preaching it now, as it
has been in Thessalonica (II Thess. 3:1). Now, we have seen plentifully
during our commentary how this was a continuous concern of Paul's and
how the whole idea was related to his judgment at the parousia. Notice how
this fear is again expressed at the end of v.2: "...for not all men have
faith—οὐ γὰρ πάντων ἡ πίστις."

(c) In spite of the opposition of the evil one (v.3), Paul is confident that the Thessalonians are abiding by his instructions (v.4) and
that consequently he will be vindicated at the parousia;

(d) Paul's prayer in v.5 is similar to that of I Thess. 3:11-13 where
the context is again that of the parousia.

Our opinion for including "καί/as well" leads us to consider v.25 not
as a general request for prayer, but rather related in its intention to
vv.23-24. The Apostle is asking the Thessalonians in this verse to pray
for him (and his companions) the same kind of prayer he did for their
sake in the two preceding verses.

vv.26-27. Ἀσπάσασθε τοὺς ἀδελφοὺς
πάντας ἐν φιλήματι ἁγίῳ. Ἐνορ-
κίζω ὑμᾶς τὸν κύριον ἀναγνωσθῆ-
ναι τὴν ἐπιστολὴν πᾶσιν τοῖς
ἀδελφοῖς.

Greet/Embrace all the brethren with a holy
kiss. I adjure you by the Lord that this letter
be read to all the brethren.

Greeting one another with a kiss is a sign of friendship[33]
or brotherhood. Here again is another instance that shows
how the early church used given human ways and poured into
them a new content. The embrace remained apparently the
same, yet a drastic change has taken place: the kiss is holy.
The faithful were indeed brethren, but this their brotherhood
was the work of the Holy Spirit (see our comments on the
words "ἀδελφοί—brethren" and "ἠγαπημένοι—beloved"
in v.1:4). He is the one who makes the kiss holy, as He
sanctifies every aspect of the life of the church.

The expression "φίλημα ἅγιον—holy kiss" seems to have
been common in the early church. Paul uses it commonly at
the end of his letters without any further comment (Rom.
16:16; I Cor. 16:20; II Cor. 13:12). Besides, we find it in
I Pet. 5:14 which reads: "Greet one another with the kiss
of peace."

Then the Apostle adjures the Thessalonians by the Lord
that his letter be read to all the brothers. Now, we have
already shown at the end of our comments on 1:1 that
Paul's epistles were meant to be read in the presence of

---

[33]Note that "φίλημα—kiss" has the same root as "φίλος—friend" and
"φιλέω—to love."

the whole community. This is further confirmed here by the use of the verb "ἀναγιγνώσκω—to read" which has the connotation of reading aloud. Anyway, this was the rule in those days when the printing press did not exist and making one copy of a manuscript took much time even at the hand of skilled scribes.

This being the case, why then would Paul adjure—the only instance in all hs epistles!—the Thessalonians that his letter be read to all the brothers? The answer can lie only in the adjective "all—πᾶσιν." The Apostle wanted to be sure that all the faithful, including the fainthearted and the weak[34] (v.14), as well as the irreverent—and perhaps dissident[35]— ones and the unruly who might have been boycotting the gatherings.

This last point might lead us to conclude that the holy kiss was a liturgical act. We just saw that the key word in v.27 is "πᾶσιν—all." This seems to be also the case in v.26. To be sure, in his other epistles Paul uses the straightforward expression "Greet one another—ἀλλήλους—with a holy kiss" (Rom. 16:16; I Cor. 16:20; II Cor. 13:12), which was actually the usual one as it appears from I Pet. 5:14. Thus, the emphasis in our verse is on that the holy kiss had to include all the brethren.[36]

In I Pet. 5:14 this holy kiss is defined as being a kiss of peace. Anyone familiar with the liturgy of the church will immediately notice that this habit has been kept at the level of the celebrants, when they embrace each other after they hear the deacon's exhortation: "Let us *love* one another so that in one mind/accord we may confess." Indeed, this love produces the oneness of mind—ὁμόνοια— without which the one faith of the church could not be expressed. That this kiss of love is the kiss of peace is reflected in the immediately following dialogue.

---

[34]Those who might have lost faith or at least hope because of the delay of the parousia.

[35]Refusing to listen to the remonstrances of the leaders to take up again their manual work to ensure their livelihood.

[36]In the Greek text "πάντες—all" is after "τοὺς ἀδελφοὺς—the brethren," which is a sign of emphasis. It is as if Paul wanted to say: "Greet the brethren, all of them, with a holy kiss."

> Deacon: Let us stand aright, let us stand with fear,
> let us attend: that we may offer the Holy
> Oblation in *peace*.
> Choir : A mercy of *peace*, a sacrifice of praise.

v.28. Ἡ χάρις τοῦ κυρίου ἡμῶν Ἰησοῦ
Χριστοῦ μεθ᾽ ὑμῶν. [Ἀμὴν]

The grace of our Lord Jesus Christ be with
you. [Amen]

Paul ends his letter with the same note with which he
started: asking that the grace of the Lord Jesus Christ be
with the Thessalonians. The mention here of the Lord Jesus
without God the Father indicates, as we showed in 1:1, the
specificity of the community: it is a Christian one.

As we said regarding [Amen] in 3:13, the same word here might have
been original, but more probably is a liturgical addition.

APPENDICES

APPENDIX I: THE SEPTUAGINT

After the fall of Jerusalem to the Babylonians in 587 B.C. many Jews (or Judahites, *i.e.*, citizens of the Kingdom of Judah) were exiled to Babylon. However, a good number of them went in different directions: in Jer. 40-44 we read how a certain number of Jews, including the prophet Jeremiah, headed towards Egypt and stayed there. We have clear indications that Jews were later found in many cities all over the territory of the Roman Empire.

Now with the advent and conquests of Alexander the Great (late third century B.C.), Greek became the main language of the Near East. In the synagogues, the need was felt that the readings taken from the Holy Scriptures in Hebrew be translated into Greek for the common people. This habit led in time to another need, namely that of having a somewhat uniform text whereby the translator would not have to come up with an *ad hoc* translation at each gathering. Such an effort materialized in Alexandria.

One of the many cities founded by and named after Alexander the Great was Alexandria of Egypt, founded in 332 B.C. Under the Ptolemies, successors of Alexander who ruled Egypt, it grew into one of the three major cities of the Roman Empire. The other two were Rome and Antioch. The latter was founded in 300 B.C. by Seleucus I and named after his father Antiochus; it was the capital of the Seleucids, successors of Alexander who ruled Syria. However, it is Alexandria that became the greatest intellectual center and cultural capital of the Hellenistic world. Moreover, it counted what was probably the largest concentration of Jews at that time. With this combination of factors it is easy to understand why it was precisely in Alexandria that the translation of the Old Testament into Greek took place, starting in the mid-third century B.C.

Since at that time the concept of scriptural canon was not yet clarified, this translation included all the main Hebrew writings which were at honor among the Jews, as well as some Jewish works that were produced directly in Greek. No wonder that such translation became widespread in the synagogues of the Hellenistic world and later of the Roman Empire. The apostles as well as the New Testament authors used it since their preaching and writings were mainly in Greek.

The place of honor and the authority this translation enjoyed in the Jewish community of the time are reflected in the legendary account of its origin extant in a work of the late second century B.C., the Letter to Aristeas. Here we read that at the request of King Ptolemy II (283-246 B.C.), who wished to have a copy of the Jewish sacred books at the library he had just founded, seventy-two elders—six from each of the twelve tribes—were sent to Alexandria. There they were put in seventy-two different cells on the island of Pharos, where they produced identical translations. The number of the elders was at the origin of the name given to this translation: Septuagint from the Latin *septuaginta*, which means seventy and is written LXX.

APPENDIX II: Κύριος - the Lord

In the Holy Scriptures the God of Abraham, Isaac and Jacob revealed His name to Moses: Yahweh (Ex. 3:13-15). One of the titles with which Yahweh was addressed, especially in invocations, *i.e.*, *'Adonai*, from the semitic *'adon* which means master, lord, and expresses the authority of the person addressed. In the LXX, this word was translated as "κύριος–lord."

Now in the Old Testament we encounter two curiosities, so to speak: one in the LXX and the other in the Hebrew text. In the Greek translation we find that the name Yahweh also is translated as κύριος. As for the Hebrew Old Testament, we notice that the vowel signs, which were introduced around the sixth century A.D.,[1] indicated that the Jews read *'Adonai* whenever the word YHWH (the four consonants of Yahweh) appeared in the text. These two oddities converge in pointing toward a fact carried on in Judaism until today: at one point of their history the Jews ceased using the sacred name Yahweh and exchanged it essentially[2] for *'Adonai*—κύριος—Lord. One of the most probable reasons is that it was too sacred to be uttered mainly among Gentiles.

---

[1]Semitic languages are essentially consonantal with no vowels. These are only signs added to help the reader.

[2]Other ways of calling God were: Heavens, Abode (*Shekinah*), the Name . . .

APPENDIX III: Χριστὸς - Christ

Christ and Messiah are English transliterations respectively of the Greek Χριστός and the Hebrew *mashiah*, both meaning the anointed one. In ancient Israel and until the fall of Jerusalem in 587 B.C., the anointed par excellence was the king. As such he was the representative of God among his people and thus a sacred person to whom religious respect was due. With the establishment of the Davidic dynasty in the southern Kingdom of Judah, all the descendants of David were considered messiahs—anointed ones. However, everyday life belied the fact that the king was indeed the representative of Yahweh. Therefore, under the influence of the prophet Isaiah (chapters 7, 9, 11), people started to look forward to and hope for a coming king who would be indeed the Messiah, the Anointed One: another David.

Such an expectation was so overwhelming in the first century A.D. that Jesus refused the title of King or Messiah whenever the crowds bestowed it readily on Him. He was afraid of their misconception of what He really was. But after His death and resurrection the apostles recognized in Him the awaited one and started calling Him Christ, to the extent that this title became another proper name for Jesus.

APPENDIX IV: Σατανᾶς - Satan

In Job 1-2 *satan* appears to be a member of the divine court acting as a prosecutor in the tribunal. The LXX often renders it by διάβολος meaning accuser or slanderer. Thus satan or the devil has become an evil angel whose main work is to tempt us and make us fall in a trap so that we be condemned. His aim is to hinder us from heading toward God by doing His will. As such he is hoping that we fail the test of trying to be on God's side and to present Him with a proof of our failure. Ultimately he proves to be the enemy of God Himself and of His work for the salvation of mankind. The Greek διάβολος, transcribed *diabolos*, has given our English word "devil."

APPENDIX V: Παρουσία - Presence/Coming

Parousia is the transliteration of the Greek noun παρουσία from the verb "πάρειμι—to be present." Yet, besides the general meaning of "presence," παρουσία meant also "coming" or "arrival" (see I Cor. 16:17; II Cor. 7:6-7; Phil. 1:26). Now, in the Hellenistic literature contemporary to Paul, parousia in the sense of coming referred specifically either to the appearance of a deity or to the official visit of an emperor, ruler or governor, or even to the official welcome given a victorious general.

The latter kind of parousia entailed an extensive paraphernalia: the preparation of the city for the joyous and glorious event, the awaiting, the clamor announcing the arrival of the visitor, the procession out of the gates to meet him, the parade bringing him into the city, his acclamation by all its inhabitants as well as his welcome, praise and glorification by the emperor.

The concept and imagery of the parousia was thus readily used in the early church to render the coming in glory of the Lord at the end of times, especially since Jesus combined in His person the threefold aspect of deity, ruler and victorious warrior over death.

INDEX OF SCRIPTURAL
REFERENCES

INDEX OF SUBJECTS

	DATE DUE	
MAY 1 1 1999		
DEC 1 5 2000		
APR 0 4 2001		
DEC 2 4 2002		
MAY 2 5 2015		
MAR 1 3 2017		

Alliance Theological Seminary
Nyack, N.Y. 10960